SEARCH AND DETECTION
4TH EDITION

ALAN R. WASHBURN

Foreward:

This book is the outgrowth of a course in Search Theory given at the Naval Postgraduate School. Students taking the course are familiar with calculus and probability, so the same is assumed of the reader. The book is not exhaustive, as is inevitable with a subject having the breadth of Search and Detection Theory. A good indication of this breadth can be obtained by comparing the material in this book with that in the references (references are given at the end of each chapter); the amount of overlap is remarkably small. Reference [5] contains an excellent bibliography, as does the more recent reference [1].

Most of the material in this book was originally motivated by military and particularly naval problems, which explains the custom of referring to the object of search as a "target". To a large extent the applications continue to be military, although there have also been applications to fishing, mineral exploration, and search and rescue [2].

The "PERT" chart on the next page shows the logical relationship among the chapters. For example, Chapter 8 can be read before any other chapter, but Chapters 2, 3, and 4 must be read before Chapter 9. The diagram errs on the side of strictness—the only loss in reading Chapter 11 first would be one of context.

A reader with access to Microsoft Excel will find it advantageous to download the workbook *Search4.xls* from the INFORMS Web site at www.informs.org/Pubs/Topics/Supplements/. Occasional references will be made to this workbook in the text.

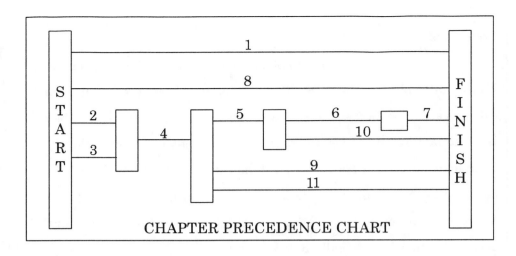

CHAPTER PRECEDENCE CHART

The apparently unsequenced Figure above is actually Figure ii because it is on page ii. This convention will be followed throughout the book. It has been adopted because it simplifies the finding of a given figure, even though it has the disadvantage that the presence of Figure ii does not imply the existence of Figure i.

Each chapter has an accompanying problem set. The answer to each problem is given when it is numerical. The author hereby offers the sum of $10 to anyone who can show that an answer is wrong, with the money going to the earliest postmark in case of multiple replies.

Thanks to Neagle Forrest for introducing me to the topic, to the U.S. Navy for its continued support, and to the intrepid Chip Boyd and other students for hopefully saving me lots of money by having found all the wrong answers already.

Alan Washburn
Code OR/Ws
Naval Postgraduate School
Monterey, CA 93943

1989 Continuation

To my surprise, there were still a few errors in the first edition, but, secure in the belief that they have all been found by now, I am doubling the reward for finding one to $20.

1996 Continuation

Additional thanks to Jim Eagle for his contributions to the third edition, and to Therese Bilodeau for beginning the typing of the third edition by scanning the second, with all that that implies.

2002 Continuation

The reward for finding an error is still $20. I am *not* doubling it because the @@##! things are costing me money!

REFERENCES

[1] Benkoski, S. J., M. G. Montesino, J. R. Weisinger. 1991. A survey of search theory literature. *Naval Res. Logist.* **38** 469–494.

[2] Haley, K. B., L. D. Stone. 1980. *Search Theory and Applications.* Plenum Press, New York.

[3] Koopman, B. O. 1980. *Search and Screening.* Pergamon Press, New York.

[4] Selin, I. 1965. *Detection Theory.* AD467769, or Princeton University Press, Princeton, NJ.

[5] Stone, L. D. 1975. *Theory of Optimal Search*, 2nd ed., INFORMS, Linthicum, MD.

[6] Stone, L. D. 1983. The process of search planning: Current approaches and continuing problems. *Oper. Res.* **31** 207-233.

Notation and Conventions

Σ means sum and Π means product; thus

$$\sum_{i=1}^{4} i = 10 \quad \text{and} \quad \prod_{i=1}^{4} i = 24.$$

When no limits are specified, Σ and Π are "over everything". When no limiting statement is made, "for all" should be understood.

$X \equiv Y$ means "equal by definition".

$P(E)$ is the probability of the event E.

$P(E \mid F)$ is the probability of the event E when the event F is given.

$E(X)$ is the expected value of the random variable X.

Section 7.3 is the third section of Chapter 7, etc.

Page 5-21 is the 21st page of Chapter 5, etc.

Figures and tables are referred to by the page on which they occur.

Angles are measured counterclockwise from "East" in radians.

References are given at the end of each chapter.

TABLE OF CONTENTS

1. OPTIMAL SEARCH PATHS

It is natural to expect that a subject called "Search Theory" will be mainly preoccupied with assessing the consequences of following a particular search path, and perhaps even with discovering paths that are in some sense optimal for the searcher. This is not the case—such problems are rare in Search Theory, and are considered only in this chapter and to a small extent in Chapters 6 and 8. It is only recently [3] that computers have become fast enough to offer the hope of finding search paths that are at least close to being optimal in general circumstances. The object of interest in this book is more likely to be a distribution of effort, the subject of Chapters 5 and 6. Nonetheless, it is appropriate to begin with some examples of classical "path problems". In all of the following examples, the sensor is of the cookie-cutter or definite range type, by which is meant that there is a fixed detection range R such that the target will be detected at the first moment when its distance from the searcher is smaller than R. This assumption is made in the hope of keeping the analysis simple. This hope will be seen to be vain; in fact, one of the reasons for emphasizing distribution of effort problems in the sequel is that they tend to be simpler than path problems.

1.1. Exhaustive Search of a Region

Consider a searcher with "sweepwidth" W, which for the moment means that the searcher sees everything within $W/2$ of his own position, and nothing beyond that. If the searcher has speed V, then VW is the rate at which area is covered. In exhaustive search, it is assumed that there is never any overlap of one searched segment with another, and no search effort is placed outside the search region. A region with area A will then be completely searched in time A/VW. Furthermore, if T is the time at which the stationary target is first detected, and if the target is equally likely to be anywhere in the region, then T is a uniform random variable over the interval $[0, A/VW]$, and the expected value of T is $E(T) = (1/2)A/VW$.

There are several ways of performing an exhaustive search. Among these are the back and forth or "raster scan" method, the "spiral-in" method, and the "spiral-out" method. Given the assumption that the target is stationary and equally likely to be anywhere, all methods are equivalent. However, it can be said that the raster scan method involves the simplest navigation, that the spiral-out method is advantageous if the target is more likely to be at the center of the spiral than in other places, and that the spiral-in method is capable of "trapping" a slowly moving target (Section 1.5).

Exhaustive search should be thought of as an upper bound on the effectiveness of searching a region. One of the reasons for this is seen in Figure 1-2 (by convention this is the figure on page 1-2), which illustrates that the requirement of path continuity forces gaps and/or overlaps in the search pattern. There are two interesting geometric questions that one

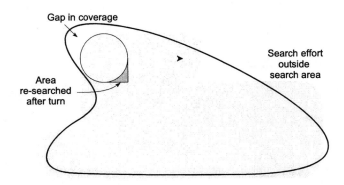

EXHAUSTIVE SEARCH OF A REGION

can pose about search in a given region:

- What is the smallest amount of track length required to cover the region completely?

- What is the largest amount of track length that can be contained inside the region without overlap?

Both questions are difficult to answer exactly, but the exhaustive search answer A/W is approximately correct provided the radius of curvature of the boundary is large compared to W. This answer is optimistic in the sense that it is too small for the first question and too large for the second.

1.2.   The Circle Packing Problem

Suppose that search is carried out by a sequence of "looks", each of which covers a circle of radius R. The circles can be placed anywhere, but are limited in number. Since the plane cannot be covered with nonoverlapping circles, there is necessarily a tradeoff between efficiency and completeness of coverage.

Figure 1-3 shows an attempt to cover the plane by packing circles of radius R into a triangular lattice. Everything except the small darkened

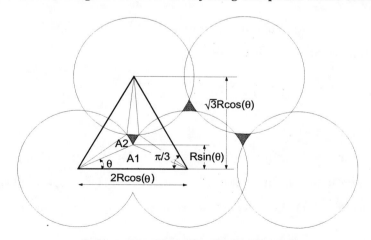

THE CIRCLE PACKING PROBLEM

1-3

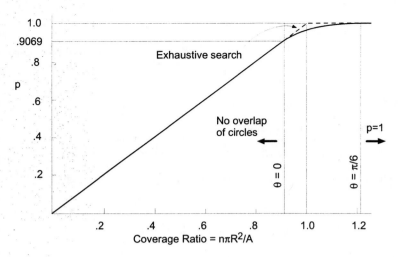

CIRCLE PACKING EFFICIENCY

areas is covered. The equilateral triangle shown is a repeating element, so the fraction of the plane covered is the same as the fraction of the triangle covered. The area of the equilateral triangle is $(1/2)$ $(2R \cos\theta)(\sqrt{3} R \cos\theta) = \sqrt{3} R^2 \cos^2\theta$. The covered area $3A_1 + 3A_2$ within it is everything but the small, darkened section at the center, where

$$A_1 = \text{area of triangle} = (1/2) \ (2R \cos\theta) \ (R \sin\theta) =$$
$$= R^2 \sin\theta \cos\theta$$

and $\qquad A_2 = \text{area of circular segment} = R^2 \ (\pi/3 - 2\theta)/2.$

The fraction of the triangle covered is

$$p = \frac{\pi/2 + 3(\sin\theta\cos\theta - \theta)}{\sqrt{3}\cos^2\theta} \qquad (1.2\text{-}1)$$

as long as $0 \le \theta \le \pi/6$.

If a large but finite region of area A is to be covered with a pattern that has characteristic angle θ, then the number of circles required will be $n = A/(2\sqrt{3} R^2 \cos^2\theta)$, ignoring edge effects, since there are twice as many triangles as circles. If n is given, we can solve for θ as long as $A/(2\sqrt{3}\,R^2\cos^2(\theta)) \le n \le A/(2\sqrt{3}\,R^2\cos^2(\pi/6))$. The circles do not overlap if n is smaller than the lower limit, and coverage is complete if n exceeds the upper limit. If the circles do not overlap, then the fraction of the region covered will be $p = n\pi R^2/A$. Figure 1-4 shows p as a function of $n\pi R^2/A$. The "exhaustive search" approximation would be $p = \min(1, n\pi R^2/A)$, which is for most purposes an adequate approximation to Figure 1-4. The smallest coverage ratio for which $p = 1$ is $2\pi/(3\sqrt{3}) = 1.209$, so about 20% of the coverage will be wasted in paving the plane with circles.

1.3.   Patrolling a Channel

Suppose that a stream of targets moves along an infinitely long channel at speed U, and that a searcher moves at speed V relative to the same channel. If the width of the channel is L and the detection range of the searcher is R, then how should the searcher patrol, and what is the resulting fraction of targets detected? It may be convenient to imagine that the targets are embedded at random places on an endless tape that has width L and speed U, in which case the fraction of targets detected is the same as the fraction of the tape covered by a disk of radius R centered on the searcher (see Figure 1-6). The same analysis applies to a single target if there is no basis on which to predict its time of arrival.

The answer depends on what other constraints are placed on searcher motion. The most common constraint is that the average searcher velocity should be zero, since this corresponds to an aircraft patrolling from a fixed base that must be returned to periodically. Here we will be somewhat more general by requiring the searcher's average velocity in the direction opposite U (to the right in Figure 1-6) to be H, where $|H| \le V$. This might be because of the need to screen an object that

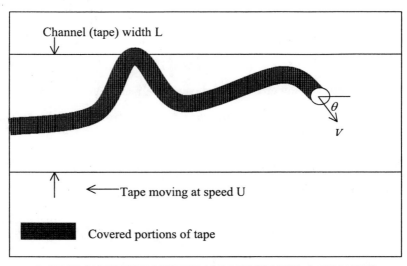

Channel (tape) width L

θ

V

Tape moving at speed U

Covered portions of tape

A SEARCHER WITH SPEED V PATROLLING A CHANNEL

moves at speed H, hence the need for a moving barrier. If $H=0$, we have the fixed barrier case.

The fixed barrier case was studied extensively in World War II [4], one of the objectives being to compute the detection probability when the searcher's horizontal motion is zero at all times—the "back-and-forth" case—and to compare this with other kinds of searcher motion. There are a distressingly large number of possible searcher motions, since any closed curve will have a velocity that is zero on the average. It is not even obvious whether the searcher's coverage disk should partially go outside the channel on occasion, as illustrated in Figure 1-6. In World War II, the need for simple patrol patterns was used to limit the number of possible closed curves subject to analysis. Here we will instead derive an upper bound that applies to all closed curves. Geometrically, this upper bound is obtained by imagining that that edges of the tape are pasted together to make a tube, an operation that favors the searcher because he can repetitively patrol around the tube without fear of the overlap that happens with a back-and-forth patrol. There is evidence [5] that this upper bound is actually quite sharp, in the sense that there exists a closed curve that comes close to achieving the upper bound. The derivation is still somewhat unsatisfying in not providing explicit instructions about how the upper bound can be (nearly) achieved, but see [4,5,6].

Let $\theta(t)$ be the searcher's course at time t, so that $V\cos(\theta(t))$ is the velocity in the direction opposite to U. Since the searcher's average velocity in this direction must be H, it follows that the average value of $V\cos(\theta(t))$ must be H. For brevity in this section we will use $<>$ to indicate an average value, so that $< V\cos(\theta(t)) >=H$.

The searcher's speed relative to the tape is

$$w(t) = \sqrt{V^2 + U^2 + 2UV\cos(\theta(t))}\,. \tag{1.3-1}$$

Since $w(t)$ is a concave function of $V\cos(\theta(t))$, $<w(t)>$ cannot exceed the quantity obtained by replacing $V\cos(\theta(t))$ in (1.3-1) by its average H. This follows from Jensen's inequality. Therefore

$$< w(t) > \le \sqrt{V^2 + U^2 + 2UH}\,. \tag{1.3-2}$$

In practice the searcher will need to worry about covering parts of the tape that have already been covered, but in any case the rate at which he covers virgin tape area cannot exceed $2R<w(t)>$, the product of sweepwidth and speed. The rate at which virgin tape area appears in the vicinity of the searcher is $L(H+U)$ as long as that quantity is postive. The fraction of the tape covered cannot exceed the ratio of these two rates, so

$$p \le \min\left\{1, \frac{2R\sqrt{V^2 + U^2 + 2UH}}{L(H+U)}\right\}; |H| \le V, H+U > 0\,. \tag{1.3-3}$$

This is the upper bound on probability of detection mentioned above. The min{} function simply assures that the bound is a probability, since the rate ratio may very well exceed 1.

It was mentioned earlier that (1.3-3) is usually sharp. Part of the reason may be that only $\cos(\theta(t))$ is referred to in the derivation. The cosine function is insensitive to the sign of its argument, so the searcher still has complete freedom as to the sign of $\theta(t)$ in determing the best track to follow.

1.4. Offset Circle Probabilities

Let X and Y be independent, normal random variables each with zero mean and standard deviation σ. The joint probability density function of (X, Y) is then

$$f(x,y) = \frac{1}{2\pi\sigma^2} \exp\left[-\left(x^2 + y^2\right)/2\sigma^2\right].$$

It often happens that the random variable $R = \sqrt{(X-h)^2 + Y^2}$ is of interest, where h is a constant. For example:

- If (X, Y) represents the random position of a target relative to a fix, and if h is the distance from the fix to a sensor or weapon, then R is the distance from the weapon or sensor to the target.

- Suppose that a target has an initial location (X, Y) relative to a fix, and then moves a distance h in a uniformly random direction. Then R represents the final distance of the target from the fix, with the bearing from the fix being uniformly random. The formula for R has the target moving an amount $(-h,0)$, but this is no restriction because the density $f(x,y)$ is radially symmetric.

Let $F_R(r) = P(R \le r)$ be the cumulative distribution function of R. The event $R \le r$ happens if and only if $(X - h, Y)$ lies in a circle C of radius r about the fix:

$$F_R(r) = \iint\limits_C \frac{1}{2\pi\sigma^2} \exp\left\{-\left[(x+h)^2 + y^2\right]\middle/2\sigma^2\right\} dx\,dy. \qquad (1.4\text{-}1)$$

Changing to polar coordinates, with $x = z\sigma\cos\theta$ and $y = z\sigma\sin\theta$,

$$F_R(r) = \int\limits_0^{r/\sigma} \int\limits_0^{2\pi} \frac{1}{2\pi} \exp\left\{-\left[z^2 + (h/\sigma)^2 + 2z(h/\sigma)\cos\theta\right]\middle/2\right\} z\,dz\,d\theta. \qquad (1.4\text{-}2)$$

Let $a = r/\sigma$ and $b = h/\sigma$ be dimensionless versions of the radius and the offset, respectively. The integral in 1.4-2 cannot be evaluated in closed form unless $b = 0$, in which case it is $1 - \exp(-a^2/2)$; this elementary formula simplifies calculations for repeated, independent attempts to cover a target. An interactive graph of 1.4-2 can be found on the "Bessel" sheet of *Search4.xls*.

The density function $f_R(r)$ can be obtained by differentiating 1.4-2. The result is

$$\sigma f_R(r) = a \exp\left[-(a^2 + b^2)\middle/2\right]\left[\frac{1}{2\pi}\int\limits_0^{2\pi} \exp(-ab\cos\theta)\,d\theta\right]$$

or

$$\sigma f_R(r) = a \exp\left[-(a^2 + b^2)\middle/2\right]I_0(ab), \qquad (1.4\text{-}3)$$

where I_0 is a Bessel function [2].

Now consider the second example where $h = Ut$, with U being the speed of the target and t being the time after the fix when a searcher arrives on scene. The searcher would be interested in the two-dimensional density function of the final Cartesian position of the target, since the peaks of that function correspond to the most productive areas to search. Since the target's bearing from the fix is random, this density function depends only on the distance from the origin r, and is therefore equal to $f_R(r)/(2\pi r)$. Figure 1-10 shows that the density function has a maximum at about $r = Ut$ when t is large (or equivalently $a = b$ when b is large). When t is smaller than σ/U, however, the probability density is highest at the origin.

A searcher with speed V who searches in such a manner that his range from the fix is always Ut will leave a track that is a logarithmic spiral. Modified spiral searches are discussed in [4].

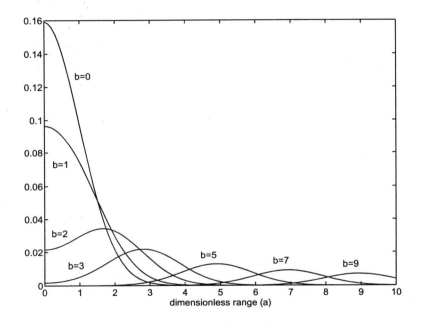

DENSITY PER UNIT AREA VERSUS RANGE FROM FIX

1.5. Trapping Circles and Spirals

Figure 1-11 portrays a situation where a mobile target is known to be somewhere inside the large circle, and must be "trapped" by a mobile searcher currently at the center of the small circle. The radius R of the small circle is a detection radius, and the question is, "Is there some way for the searcher to maneuver such that his distance from the target must eventually be $\leq R$, regardless of how the target moves?" Equivalently, the question is "Does a trapping maneuver exist?" The portrayed situation typically arises when the target commits some act at the center of the large circle (hereafter the "datum") that attracts the searcher from far away. If the target's speed is U, then Figure 1-11 shows the situation at the earliest time t_0 at which detection is conceivable, with t_0 depending on how far away the searcher was to begin with. The searcher's speed V is assumed to be larger than U.

One example of a trapping maneuver is a trapping circle with radius $Ut_0 + R$ about the datum. The time required to complete one cycle is $2\pi(Ut_0 + R)/V$. If the target cannot move as much as the sweepwidth $2R$ during that time, then it is essentially trapped within Ut_0 of the origin. The criterion for trapability is thus $\pi(Ut_0 + R)/V < R/U$, or

$$t_0 < (R/U)\left(\frac{V}{\pi U} - 1\right). \qquad (1.5\text{-}1)$$

The strict inequality in (1.5-1) permits the searcher to gradually spiral inward until detection occurs, assuming endurance permits.

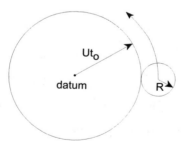

INITIAL CONFIGURATION AND TRAPPING CIRCLE

The largest value of t_0 for which there exists a trapping maneuver is unknown. If it is not possible for the searcher to trap the target, the question still arises as to how the searcher should maneuver so as to maximize the probability of detection. One approximate model for that situation is discussed in Section 2.3.

1.6.   The Effect of Counter-Detection

Consider a searcher with detection range R and speed V who is searching for a target with counterdetection range S and speed U. We assume in this section that the dimensionless ratio $\beta \equiv R/S$ is smaller than 1, since otherwise the target will be detected before he has a chance to react to the searcher. We also assume that the dimensionless ratio $\alpha \equiv U/V$ is smaller than 1, so the searcher is faster than the target, and that the searcher's course is fixed throughout the engagement and known to the target. This latter assumption may be false if the searcher is free to choose a random, sinuous course (see Section 2.5), but could be accurate if the searcher were actually a towed device such as a fish net [1]. In any case, the problem is to derive an equivalent sweepwidth W_e under these assumptions.

It is convenient to adopt a reference system centered on the searcher, in which case a drift of magnitude V toward the searcher must be superimposed on the target's motion. If the target's velocity has an angle θ with respect to the searcher's course, then the two components of the target's velocity relative to the searcher are $V - U \cos\theta$ horizontally and $U \sin\theta$ vertically. The resulting track of the target will be such that (see Figure 1-13)

$$\tan\phi = U \sin\theta / (V - U \cos\theta)$$
$$= \alpha \sin\theta / (1 - \alpha \cos\theta). \tag{1.6-1}$$

The target wants to make ϕ as large as possible. Let ϕ^* be the largest possible value of ϕ. It can be shown by differentiation that the maximizing angle θ^* is such that

$$\cos\theta^* = \alpha, \tag{1.6-2}$$

in which case

$$\sin\phi^* = \alpha. \tag{1.6-3}$$

The closest point of approach of target to searcher is $S\sin(\psi + \phi^*)$, so the target will be detected if and only if $S\sin(\psi + \phi^*) \leq R$. The largest angle ψ^* for which this is true can be obtained from

$$\sin(\psi^* + \phi^*) = \beta. \tag{1.6-4}$$

If $\alpha > \beta$, the target can escape even if it initially lies directly on the path of the searcher, and therefore $W_e = 0$. Otherwise 1.6-4 has a solution for ψ^* in

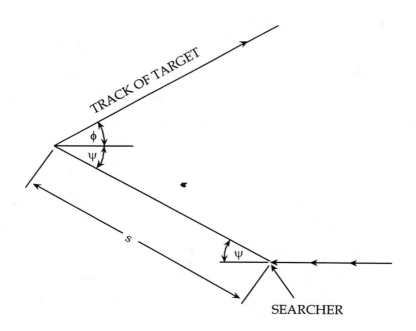

TRACK OF TARGET RELATIVE TO SEARCHER

the interval $[0, \pi/2 - \phi^*]$. The target will be detected if and only if it lies initially within $S \sin\psi^*$ of the searcher's track, so the equivalent sweepwidth W_e when $\alpha \leq \beta$ is

$$W_e = 2S \sin\psi^*. \qquad (1.6\text{-}5)$$

The equivalent sweepwidth will never be larger than $2R$.

Avoidance Example.

$R = 1$, $S = 2$, $V = 10$, $U = 2$. The equivalent sweepwidth can be obtained by first solving 1.6-3 ($\phi^* = .201$ radians), then 1.6-4 ($\psi^* = .322$ radians), and then 1.6-5 ($W_e = 1.27$). Note that W_e is considerably smaller than $2R$; the effect of even small evasion speeds is substantial.

A similar analysis can be performed for the case where the target desires to approach the searcher, rather than avoid him. This may either be because the target hopes to be rescued by the searcher, or because the target seeks the searcher's destruction. In the latter case, the names of the two parties might well be interchanged, but the essential fact in either case is that the target desires proximity. Analytically, the only difference from the case where the target avoids the searcher is that the target now makes the sign of ϕ negative, the effect being that the track of the target in Figure 1-13 points toward the searcher, rather than away from him. The negative angle $\phi*$ is now the solution of 1.6-3, but with the sign reversed. Since $\phi*$ is negative, it is possible that the solution of 1.6-4 for ψ^* will exceed $\pi/2$. This will happen if and only if $\alpha^2 + \beta^2 > 1$. The equivalent sweepwidth in these cases is simply $2S$, since they correspond to situations where the target need not begin his approach until the searcher is already past. As long as $\alpha^2 + \beta^2 \leq 1$, the equivalent sweepwidth is given by 1.6-5.

Approach Example.

$R = 1$, $S = 2$, $V = 10$, $U = 2$. The equivalent sweepwidth can be obtained by first solving 1.6-3 and reversing the sign ($\phi^* = -.201$ radians), then 1.6-4 ($\psi^* = .725$ radians), and then 1.6-5 ($W_e = 2.65$). Note that W_e is now larger than $2R$.

1.7   Sprint and Drift

There are sensors for which search is inherently discontinuous. The classic example is use of a dipping sonar by a helicopter. The helicopter must hover while the sonar is wet, and the sonar must be dry (retracted) when the helicopter moves. Searching with such a sensor must consist of a sequence of looks separated by movement. Other searchers might be wise to imitate such tactics even though continuous search is possible. One reason for this might be that the detection range R is very small when moving due to self-noise, but much larger when stopped. Predators and prey alike will often pause to look and listen for this reason. Another reason might be the possibility of evasive motion by the target if counterdetections at range S happen as in Section 1.6. In order to counter such evasive motion, the searcher might be wise to turn off his active sensor and proceed quietly for periods, hoping to surprise the target when the sensor is suddenly turned on. All of these tactics are referred to as "sprint and drift", with the sprint part being devoted to motion without detection and the drift part to detection without motion.

We assume here that V, R and S are as in Section 1.6, but that U is infinite; that is, there is no hope of detecting the target (or any target) whose position happens to be in the annulus between R and S. The only hope of detection is if the target is within R of the sensor at the start of one of its drift periods. The length of a drift period ("look") is an input τ, and the object to be sought is the optimal sprint distance X. The sensor can always avoid the possibility of counterdetection by moving at least $R + S$ between looks, but moving a somewhat smaller distance will increase the amount of area covered (in the sense of detecting any contained targets) per unit time. We assume that the goal is to maximize this area coverage rate.

If the searcher moves a distance that is slightly smaller than $R + S$, he will cover all of the area that is inside a small circle of radius R but outside of a large circle of radius S, on each look, the previous look having ruined the rest of the small circle. In Figure 1-17, the area covered is $A \equiv A_2 + A_3$. Let Y be the height of the triangle formed by the segments labeled S and R and the horizontal axis, and let X be the base. Then A_1 and A_3 are circular segments and $A_1 + A_2 = XY$, so A can be determined once X and Y are known. The optimal tactic is most easily found by searching for the best height Y in the interval $[0,R]$, with the relevant formulas being

$$\sin(r) = Y / S \text{ and } A_1 = rS^2$$
$$\sin(s) = Y / R \text{ and } A_3 = (\pi - s)R^2$$
$$X = R\cos(s) + S\cos(r) \qquad (1.7\text{-}1)$$
$$A = A_3 + XY - A_1$$
$$\text{coverage rate} = A / (\tau + X / V).$$

If there is no danger of evasion due to counterdetection, set $S=R$.

Sheet "SprntDrft" of *Search4.xls* automates and illustrates 1.7-1.

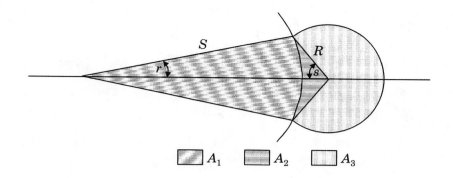

$$\boxed{A_1} \; A_1 \qquad \boxed{} \; A_2 \qquad \boxed{} \; A_3$$

EACH LOOK WILL FIND TARGETS IN A₂+A₃

Example.

Suppose $\tau=.1$, $R=5$, $S=7$, and $V=20$. Then exhaustive search on Y shows that the optimal value is about 3, corresponding to $s=.64$ radians, $r=.44$ radians and $X=10.32$. Area covered per unit time is then 116.39. A searcher who moved $R+S=12$ in order to make counterdetection impossible would have to settle for a coverage rate of only 112.20, slightly smaller than the maximum possible value.

CHAPTER 1. <u>Exercises</u>

1. Suppose that 10 searchers with sweepwidth 1 mile are available for stationary (H=0) patrol of a channel of width 20 miles, with $V = U$.

   a) If the 10 searchers are able to act as a single searcher with a 10-mile sweepwidth, approximately what would the probability of detection be?

   b) If each searcher patrols independently of the others, approximately what would be the probability that at least one searcher detects the target?

   ANSWER: .71, .52.

2. If a searcher with speed zero were required to patrol a channel with a stationary barrier, it is intuitively clear that the best possible detection probability is 1 if $2R$ exceeds L, or otherwise $2R/L$, since the searcher can do no better than just sitting in the middle of the channel. There are some cases other than V=0 and H=0 where (1.3-3) reduces to this quantity. Show that one of them is where V=H, and explain in words why no searcher could improve on the bound in this case.

3. If the radius r of a circular target is 100 yards, and if the delivery inaccuracy σ is 200 yards, what is the probability of hitting the target? What is the probability of hitting the target at least once in 10 independent tries? Assume no offset.

   ANSWER: .12, .71.

4. A searcher with speed 30 knots is looking for targets with speed 5 knots. The searcher can detect targets at 20 miles using active sonar or 5 miles using passive sonar. The counterdetection range for active

sonar is 60 miles, but of course the use of passive sonar cannot be detected. If the assumptions of Section 1.6 hold, and if sweepwidth is the criterion, which type of sonar is better?

ANSWER: W_e = 20.6 miles for active sonar, which exceeds the 10-mile passive sweepwidth. So active sonar is better. This conclusion is strongly sensitive to target speed.

5. Consider the counterdetection model of Section 1.6, assuming that the target is a lost person who wants to maximize the effective sweepwidth. It is common for the target of a search to detect the searcher long before the searcher detects the target, so suppose R = 2 miles, S = 10 miles, V = 100 miles per hour, and U = 4 miles per hour. What is the resulting effective sweepwidth, assuming that the target moves optimally?

ANSWER: 4.78 miles.

6. Section 1.6 includes the assertion that the equivalent sweepwidth in the approaching case when $\alpha^2 + \beta^2 > 1$ is $2S$. Prove that this is the case.

7. If the example of Section 1.7 is changed so that R = 6, what is the optimal sprint distance, and what is the optimized coverage rate? Use sheet "SprntDrft" of *Search4.xls*.

PARTIAL ANSWER: The optimal coverage rate is 160.23.

REFERENCES

[1] Barkley, R.A. 1964. The theoretical effectiveness of towed net samplers as related to sampler size and to swimming speed of organisms. *Conseil Internat. Explor. Mer* **29** 146–157.

[2] *Handbook of Mathematical Functions. 1965.* National Bureau of Standards Applied Math. Series 55, Third Printing, Formula 9.2.20.

[3] Kierstead, D., D. DelBalzo. 2001. A genetic algorithm approach for planning search paths in complicated environments. *Military Oper. Res.* Forthcoming.

[4] Koopman, B.O. 1980. *Search and Screening.* Pergamon Press, New York.

[5] Washburn, A.R. 1976. Patrolling a channel revisited. Naval Postgraduate School Report NPS55Ws75121.

[6] Washburn, A.R. 1982. On patrolling a channel. *Naval Res. Logist.* **29** 609–615.

2. MODELS BASED ON DETECTION RATE

Models such as those covered in Chapter 1 are sometimes disappointing in practice, particularly when they predict large probabilities of detection. There are several reasons for this, some of which are listed below:

a) The models all use the "cookie cutter" detection rule, whereas it is often the case that there is no definite region such that detection is certain within the region and impossible outside it.

b) Real world navigation is not perfect. The plan and execution of a particular search pattern may turn out to be substantially different things. This is particularly true if several searchers are involved.

c) The target may purposely or inadvertently foil a carefully laid plan by moving around while the search is being carried out.

The detection rate approach to computation of detection probabilities has proved to be more robust than the geometric models of Section 1 in the face of difficulties such as those mentioned above. The idea is to replace specific assumptions about placement of search effort with a probabilistic assumption of independence.

2.1. General Development

We assume that at every time u there is a "detection rate" $\gamma(u)$ with the properties that

a) $\Delta\gamma(u)$ is the probability of detection in a small time interval of length Δ that includes u.

b) the events of detection in non-overlapping time intervals are all independent.

Assumptions a) and b) determine the probability $p(t)$ that detection will occur somewhere in the interval $[0,t)$. To show this, let $q(t) = 1 - p(t)$. Then

$$q(t + \Delta) = q(t)\,(1 - \gamma(t)\Delta), \tag{2.1-1}$$

since the events of no detection over the intervals $[0,t)$ and $[t, t + \Delta)$ are independent. Therefore,

$$\frac{q(t + \Delta) - q(t)}{\Delta} = -q(t)\gamma(t). \tag{2.1-2}$$

Taking the limit as Δ approaches 0, we obtain

$$\frac{d}{dt}q(t) = -q(t)\gamma(t). \tag{2.1-3}$$

The solution of this differential equation is

$$q(t) = \exp(-n(t)), \quad \text{where} \quad n(t) = \int_0^t \gamma(u)\,du. \tag{2.1-4}$$

There is a useful interpretation of $n(t)$. Normally, one imagines that the detection process stops at the first detection, if there is one, in the interval $[0,t)$. Consider an experiment, however, where the searcher continues to repeatedly detect the target (assume no difference between alerted and unalerted detections), and let $N(t)$ be the random number of times detection occurs up to time t. Then the mean of $N(t)$ is just $n(t)$, which justifies use of the term "detection rate" for $\gamma(u)$. More precisely, $N(t)$ is a Poisson random variable with probability law

$$P(N(t) = k) = \frac{(n(t))^k}{k!}\exp(-n(t)),$$

and $q(t)$ is just $P(N(t) = 0)$. If the detection process stops at the first detection, then only the events $N(t) = 0$ and $N(t) \geq 1$ can be distinguished, but it is still conceptually useful to remember that $n(t)$ in 2.1-4 is just the mean of $N(t)$.

A random variable that is often of interest is the time T until detection first occurs. The tail distribution of T is $q(t) = p(T > t)$. For nonnegative random variables like T, the mean $E(T)$ is the area under the tail distribution, so

$$E(T) = \int_0^\infty q(t)dt. \tag{2.1-5}$$

The reader should note that in deriving Formulas 2.1-4 and 2.1-5, we have at no time given any instructions as to how such a search could actually be carried out, or even dealt with the question of whether there is any way of searching such that assumption b) holds. The real justification for using 2.1-4 and 2.1-5 is empirical; the fact is that those formulas provide good approximations in a wide variety of circumstances.

2.2. Random Search versus Exhaustive Search in a Fixed Region

Consider a random search by a cookie cutter searcher with sweepwidth W in a region that has area A. If the searcher's speed is V, then in time Δ he looks at an area of size $VW\Delta$, so the probability of detection should be $(VW\Delta)/A$; i.e., $\chi(u) = VW/A$. From 2.1-4, $n(t) = VWt/A$. The resulting function $1 - q(t) = 1 - \exp(-VWt/A)$ is shown as the lowest curve in Figure 2-4, where $z = VWt/A$. In this case, the time to detection T is an exponential random variable with mean A/VW. Since T is exponential, the time remaining until the first detection occurs has the same exponential distribution regardless of how much time has already been spent searching unsuccessfully. Waiting for the first detection in a random search is in this sense like waiting for the first "head" in a series of coin flips. This lack of memory is really what characterizes random search.

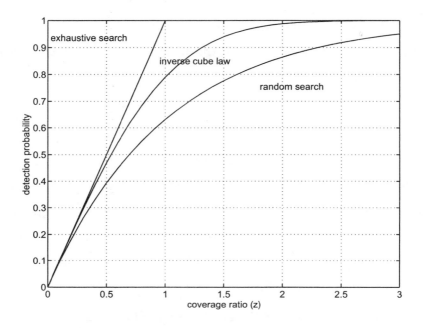

COMPARISON OF THREE SEARCH MODES

Figure 2-4 also shows probability of detection versus time for an exhaustive search (Section 1.1), as well as for an intermediate case (inverse cube law) that will be discussed in Section 2.4. For the moment, note only that exhaustive search is considerably more effective than random search. In exhaustive search, the target will be detected exactly once in the time interval $[0, A/VW]$, so there is never any need to search longer than A/VW. This is not true in random search.

Here is another comparison of the two kinds of search. Let A be the area to be covered, and let $A' = VWt$ be the area that can be searched. The exhaustive searcher places A' within A and covers a fraction A'/A, or else all of A if $A' > A$. In effect, the random searcher cuts A' into confetti and drops the confetti at random onto A. To see that this gives the correct fraction covered, let there be n pieces of confetti, each located uniformly and independently at random within A. The probability that any given piece of confetti fails to cover a particular point within A is $1 - A'/nA$. The probability that none of the n pieces of confetti cover the same point is therefore $(1 - A'/(nA))^n$, which approaches $\exp(-A'/A)$ when n is large. So random search is effectively confetti casting, and it achieves a lower detection probability than exhaustive search because of wasteful overlap of one piece of confetti on another. The complete lack of organization inherent in attempting to search by effectively casting confetti explains why random search is often treated as a lower bound in computing detection probability, even though a deliberate attempt to achieve a low detection probability (for example by not moving) could do even worse.

Random search is evidently not a goal for the searcher; the idea of trying to be completely disorganized is ridiculous. It would be a mistake to deliberately perform a random walk in order to "achieve" a random search. Nonetheless, the random search formula often provides accurate answers. Consider, for example, the following experiment: An evader is initially placed uniformly at random within a square of side L, and subsequently moves around "at random" (the exact motion being up to the evader) at speed U within the square. A much faster pursuer ($U/V = .2$) also starts at a uniformly random point, chosen independently of the evader's initial position, and searches in whatever manner he chooses for the evader at a speed V, where V is such that $L/V = 15.42$ seconds. The search ends when the searcher comes within $W/2$ of the evader, where $W/L = .0572$. What can be said about the time until detection occurs? We might consider two answers:

a) The target is essentially stationary, since U is small compared to V. The searcher should perform an exhaustive search, and the mean time to detection should be about $.5L^2/WV = .5(15.42 \text{ sec})/(.0572) = 135 \text{ sec}$.

b) The target's speed, though small, is sufficiently large to turn an "exhaustive" pattern into what is in effect a random search. Actually, it does not matter very much what the pursuer does, and the mean time to detection should be about $L^2/WV = 270 \text{ sec}$.

Figure 2-6 shows the results of actually performing the experiment 38 times in an electronic game where each player has his own CRT display and joystick control. The experimental cumulative distribution of the time to detection is compared with theoretical distributions corresponding to exhaustive and random search. The results are better explained by the latter. As mentioned earlier in 2.1, other phenomena that can turn

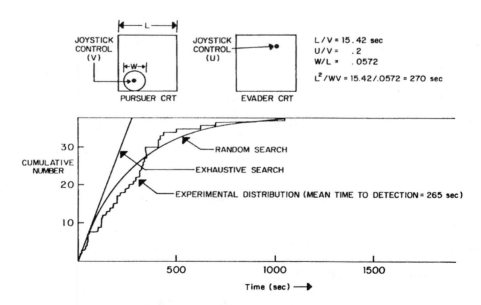

RANDOM VERSUS EXHAUSTIVE SEARCH

exhaustive searches into random searches are imperfect navigation and non cookie-cutter detection rules.

The random search formula generalizes easily to situations where there are multiple searchers and targets. For example, if the detection rate is γ when there is one searcher, then it is $n\gamma$ when there are n searchers. It is also true that the sensor need not be cookie-cutter if sweepwidth is defined as in Chapter 4. For these reasons, as well as the fundamental accuracy of the underlying independence-in-intervals assumption in many situations, the random search formula plays a central role in search theory.

2.3. Expanding Area Search for an Evader

It sometimes happens that a pursuer is given an exact position for an evader at a time when he is nowhere near the evader's position. By the time the pursuer arrives at the evader's position, an amount of time τ has passed, within which the evader may have moved. If the evader's maximum speed is U, then his position is contained in an expanding circle with radius $U(\tau + u)$ at time u after the pursuer arrives. If the pursuer moves at speed V with sweepwidth W, then the rate of covering area is VW, and the ratio of this to the expanding area is

$$\gamma(u) = \frac{VW}{\pi U^2 (\tau + u)^2} \, ; \, u \geq 0. \qquad (2.3\text{-}1)$$

If $\gamma(u)$ is taken to be the detection rate of Section 2.1, then, using 2.1-4,

$$n(t) = \int_0^t \gamma(u)du = \frac{VW}{\pi U^2}\left(\frac{1}{\tau} - \frac{1}{\tau + t}\right), \qquad (2.3\text{-}2)$$

and $q(t) = \exp(-n(t))$. An interesting feature in this case is that $n(\infty) = VW/\pi U^2 \tau$, which is finite, so $q(\infty) > 0$ and (from 2.1-5) $E(T) = \infty$.

Even if the searcher searches "forever", the probability of detection is less than 1! The reason is that the amount of area covered goes up linearly with time, whereas the area of the expanding region goes up with the square of time. If the detection is not made early, it will not be made at all.

Figure 2-8 shows the results of a video-game-like experiment where

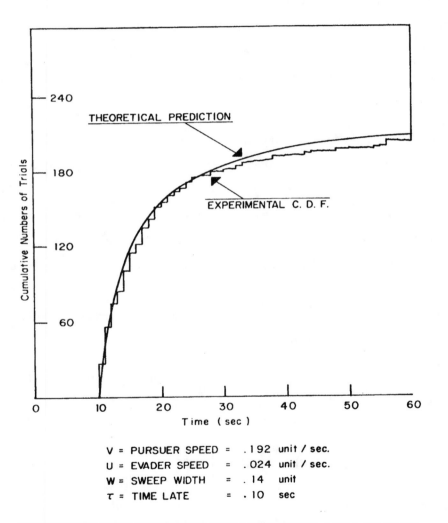

V = PURSUER SPEED = .192 unit / sec.
U = EVADER SPEED = .024 unit / sec.
W = SWEEP WIDTH = .14 unit
τ = TIME LATE = .10 sec

THEORY VERSUS EXPERIMENT IN EXPANDING AREA SEARCH

each player (a military officer) sees and controls only his own position using a joystick. In each of 295 trials, the Evader starts at the center of the screen and maneuvers for 10 seconds before the faster Pursuer (who of course cannot see the Evader's screen) begins looking for him. Capture times are recorded to the nearest second, up to at most 60 seconds. The agreement of theory with experiment is remarkable, especially since the theory relies on independence assumption b of Section 2.1, which at first seems implausible for continuously moving players. One effect of two parties maneuvering with opposite goals is that detections in non-overlapping intervals become independent of each other, which is what the theory requires. Reference [3] contains further details, not all of which are as flattering to the theory.

2.4　The Inverse Cube Law

For optical detection where atmospheric absorption can be neglected, it is reasonable to suppose that $\gamma(u)$ is proportional to the solid angle subtended by the target. For an object at range r from the sensor with apparent area A, the solid angle is A/r^2. If the target is a two-dimensional "ink blot" with area A, and if the sensor is a distance r away at a height h above the plane of the ink blot, then the apparent area of the ink blot is Ah/r for $h \ll r$, and therefore the solid angle is Ah/r^3. This ink blot or inverse cube law model was proposed in World War II [1] to explain the range at which a ship's wake could be detected.

Since the dependence of γ on range is known, probability of detection for any track of searcher relative to target can be computed or simulated. Here we compute it for the common case where the relative track is a straight line. The origin of time was arbitrary in Section 2.1, so replace 2.1-4 with

$$q(t_1,t_2) = \exp(-n(t_1,t_2)), \quad \text{where} \quad n(t_1,t_2) = \int_{t_1}^{t_2} \gamma(u)\,du, \qquad (2.4\text{-}1)$$

and where $1 - q(t_1,t_2)$ is the probability of detection over any interval $[t_1,t_2]$. In particular, if $\gamma(u) = kAh/r^3$ and if the searcher passes by the target (or vice versa) at speed V on an infinite straight line that misses the target by x, then

$$n(-\infty,\infty) = \int_{-\infty}^{\infty} \frac{kAh}{\left(h^2 + x^2 + V^2 u^2\right)^{\frac{3}{2}}}\,du$$

$$= \frac{2m}{h^2 + x^2} \qquad (2.4\text{-}2)$$

where $m = kAh/V$. The constant k accounts for the contrast of the target against its background, the quality of the sensing equipment, etc.

For long range sensors, the quantity h^2 can be neglected in the denominator of 2.4-2. The probability that detection will occur somewhere along the line is then

$$p(x) = 1 - q(-\infty,\infty) = 1 - \exp(-n(-\infty,\infty)) \qquad (2.4\text{-}3)$$
$$= 1 - \exp(-2m/x^2).$$

The function $p(x)$ is a "lateral range curve" (Chapter 4).

The associated sweepwidth W (Chapter 4) is

$$W = \int_{-\infty}^{\infty} p(x)\,dx = \sqrt{8\pi m} = \sqrt{8\pi\,kAh/V}\,. \qquad (2.4\text{-}4)$$

Note that the altitude h must be quadrupled in order to double the sweepwidth. W decreases with V, but the product VW increases with V, so high speed is beneficial in this situation.

With a cookie cutter sensor, if a region is swept in such a manner that parallel tracks are separated by a sweepwidth, then detection is certain. This is not true in the case of the inverse cube law. If the track spacing is S, probability of detection will always increase if S is decreased. To be precise, let the lateral range of the target with respect to the ith track be $x - iS$ for $i = 0, \pm 1, \pm 2, \ldots$, and assume that the detection events on the various tracks are independent. Then the probability of no detection on track i is $\exp(-2m/(x - iS)^2)$, and the probability of no detection on any track is

$$q(x,S) = \exp(-N(x,S)) \qquad (2.4\text{-}5)$$

where

$$N(x,S) = \sum_{i=-\infty}^{\infty} 2m\big/(x - iS)^2 = (\pi/4)(W/S)^2 \csc^2(\pi x/S).$$

The first equality is because exponents are added in taking a product of exponentials. The second is well known but not obvious.

Equation 2.4-5 shows in a precise manner how probability of detection increases as S decreases when the location of the target is known. In the more common circumstance where the target is located uniformly at random with respect to the tracks, the probability of detection is

$$1 - \frac{1}{S}\int_0^S q(x,S)dx = 2\Phi\left(\sqrt{\frac{\pi}{2}}\,\frac{W}{S}\right) - 1, \qquad (2.4\text{-}6)$$

where Φ is the cumulative normal function. The equality is again well known but not obvious. Since W/S can be interpreted as a coverage ratio, it is reasonable to compare 2.4-6 with the same results for exhaustive and random search. The middle curve in Figure 2-4 is Formula 2.4-6 with $z = W/S$. In this case coverage of an area by equally spaced tracks can be viewed as an attempt at exhaustive search that fails on account of the non-cookie-cutter nature of the inverse cube law sensor. Formula 2.4-6 quantifies the extent of the failure. If a searcher with an inverse cube law sensor were to search randomly, the detection probability would be given by the random search curve, rather than 2.4-6, just as it would be for a searcher with a cookie-cutter sensor. Given a random search, the only important property of a sensor is its sweepwidth.

Formulas 2.4-2, 4, 5, and 6 each involved evaluation of an infinite sum or integral. The fact that all four of these expressions can be evaluated in closed form is a circumstance so remarkable as to cause one to suspect divine interference. The inverse cube law is therefore possibly holy, and in any case deserves consideration through being a compromise between the random and exhaustive assumptions, even in circumstances where the precise assumptions lying behind it are not directly verifiable. For example, the "first search" curve in the National Search and Rescue manual [2] is just the inverse cube law, with the other curves being derived from it through an independence assumption.

Figure 2-13 shows an attempt to detect a target in the interval $[-3,3]$ using an inverse cube law sensor with $S = W = 1$. Five tracks are located at $-2, -1, 0, +1, +2$, so the figure shows 2.4-3 with $m = 1/(8\pi)$ drawn five times with solid lines. The curved dashed line shows the cumulative effect of all five sensors; the effect is substantially smaller than $q(x,1)$ on the ends because the tracks at -2 and $+2$ have no outside neighbors. The average value of the curved dashed line (approximately .67) is also shown as a flat dashed line. If there were infinitely many tracks, rather than only five, this average value would be .79, as either calculated from 2.4-6 or read from Figure 2-4 with $z = 1$. Formula 2.4-6 applies only in the limiting case; the .67 number quoted above was obtained by numerical integration.

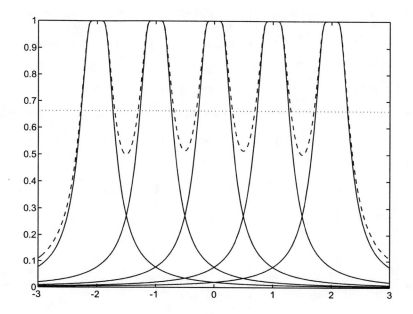

THE EFFECT OF FIVE INVERSE CUBE LAW TRACKS

2.5. Search Games

Search problems where the target can take evasive action based on the position of the searcher very seldom yield to analysis. One method of dealing with such situations is to simulate them in the manner discussed in 2.2 and 2.3. The pursuer and evader each use a joystick to manipulate the position of a "bug" on a cathode ray tube (each player having his own tube), and the game is terminated electronically when conditions for detection are met. The game is repeated often enough to derive whatever statistics about the time to detection are required.

Consider, for example, a game where the evader always knows the direction to the pursuer, but which is otherwise similar to the game discussed in 2.2—the evader is much slower than the pursuer and has to stay within a box of side L, and both players are started at uniformly random locations within the box.

Figure 2-14 shows the experimental distribution of the time to detection for 131 repetitions of the above game. Two things stand out:

a) The mean time to detection (367 seconds) is considerably greater than when the evader simply moves around at random (265 seconds in Figure 2-6).

b) The experimental distribution is very closely matched by the exponential distribution, which is the same as saying that the detection rate is constant.

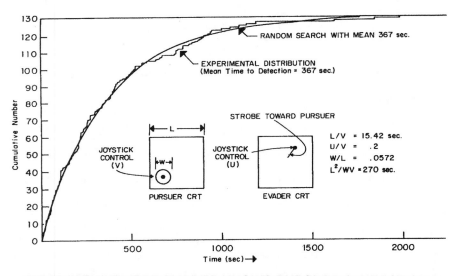

EXPERIMENT WHERE EVADER KNOWS PURSUER'S DIRECTION

Conclusion a) verifies quantitatively what was clear at the outset: an informed evader can evade detection longer than one that has to move around blindly. The quantitative nature of the result is of value only for applications where the parameters involved are scaled versions of those used in the experiment. Without benefit of any theory as to what is going on in the game, we cannot say anything about what would happen if the speed ratio were changed from .2 to .3, for example.

On the other hand, conclusion b) seems to be characteristic of search games conducted within a confined area. In a different experiment the evader was given both direction and range to the pursuer, with the parameters otherwise being the same. The mean time to detection increased to 407 seconds, but the detection rate was still constant. This tendency of the detection rate to be constant can be taken advantage of in cases where experimentation is costly, since it is easier to estimate a parameter (typically the mean time to detection) than a distribution.

There are, of course, search problems where the detection rate is not constant. The expanding area search in Section 2.3 is an example.

Chapter 2. Exercises

1. Let V, W, and A be as in Section 2.2, but suppose that there are 2 targets and 5 searchers within A, each searching randomly and independently of the others. If $V = 10$ miles/hr, $W = 1$ miles, and $A = 100$ sq. miles,

   a) If T is the first time when some target is detected by some searcher, what is $E(T)$?

   b) What fraction of the targets will have been detected by some searcher after 5 hours, on the average?

   c) What fraction of the searchers will have detected some target after 5 hours, on the average?

   ANSWER: $E(T) = 1$ hr, .92, .63.

2. Let V, W, and A be as in Section 2.2, but suppose that the searcher searches until he finds the target or until τ expires, whichever comes first.

   a) What is the probability that the search will terminate when τ expires?

   b) What is the average amount of time spent searching?

   ANSWER: $\exp(-VW\tau/A)$, $(A/VW)\,(1 - \exp(-VW\tau/A))$.

3. Consider a problem where more and more searchers continually arrive within a fixed area until the target is finally found. It might be reasonable to construct a detection rate model of such a situation with $\gamma(u) = u/\tau^2$, where τ has units of time. If this were done, what would be the formulas for $q(t)$ and $E(T)$?

   ANSWER: $q(t) = \exp(-.5t^2/\tau^2)$, $E(T) = \tau\sqrt{\pi/2}$

4. A single searcher searches randomly at speed V and sweepwidth W in an area A. There are initially n targets in A, which the searcher marks as he finds them. On the average, how long will it take the searcher to mark all n of the targets?

ANSWER: (A/VW) $[1 + 1/2 + 1/3 + ... + 1/n]$. The [   ] quantity is the first n terms of the harmonic series, which is approximately $ln(n) + .577$ for large n.

REFERENCES

[1] Koopman, B. O. 1956. The theory of search II. Target detection. *Oper. Res.* 4 503–509.

[2] National Search and Rescue Manual. 1991. JOINT PUB 3-50 and 3-50.1, Joint Chiefs of Staff, Washington, D.C.

[3] Washburn, A. R. 1980. Expanding area search experiments. Naval Postgraduate School Report NPS55-80-017.

3. DETECTION MODELS BASED
ON THE RADAR/SONAR EQUATION

3.1. Signal Excess

In many applications, detections occur through propagation of pressure (sonar) or electromagnetic (radar) waves emitted or reflected by the target. In either case, there are physical models that predict "signal excess" (e) given the relative positions of sensor and target:

$$e \equiv 10 \log_{10} (S/N) - 10 \log_{10} (S/N)_{req}. \qquad (3.1\text{-}1)$$

In Equation 3.1-1, S/N is the ratio of signal to noise power at the receiver, and $(S/N)_{req}$ is the minimum signal to noise ratio "required" for detection*. The units of e are decibels (db). If e = 10 db, 3 db, 0 db, −3 db, or −10 db, then the signal-to-noise ratio is 10, 2, 1, .5, or .1 times the ratio required for detection.

The reason why signal power is always related to noise power is that even very weak signals can be amplified electronically to be as strong as is convenient, so the absolute value of the signal is not important. However, amplification also magnifies whatever noise may be present, and this noise will mask the presence of the signal regardless of amplification if it is sufficiently strong relative to the signal. Thus, the relevant question in deciding whether any physical phenomenon can form the basis of a detection mechanism is not "How strong is it?", but rather "How strong is it relative to the noise with which it must compete?" The noise in 3.1-1 may be due to distant shipping, breaking waves, thermal agitation in a resistor, deliberate noise emitted by an opponent (jamming), or various

---

* But see Chapter 9.

other phenomena. Whatever the source, noise is the ultimate limit on detection.

3.2 Sonar Models Based on Signal Excess

The physical models used with 3.1-1 are usually sufficiently approximate that detection turns out not to be synonymous with positive signal excess. In order to make theory come closer to agreeing with reality, it is therefore sometimes assumed that signal excess E is actually a random variable, normally distributed with mean e and variance σ^2. The probability of detection is then $P(E > 0) = \Phi(e/\sigma)$, where Φ is the cumulative normal distribution and σ is whatever number of decibels makes theory and practice come closest to agreeing. Most practitioners use a value of σ somewhere between 3 and 9 db for sonar detection in the ocean; since 3 db is a factor of 2, 9 db is a factor of 8. A Monte Carlo simulation of detections would be quite simple with this model: first, employ some sort of physical model to predict e, then subtract X which is normal with mean zero and variance σ^2 to obtain E, and then declare that a detection has occurred if and only if $E > 0$.

The idea of introducing a standard deviation σ that essentially represents the inaccuracy of the radar or sonar equation may seem to be a practical, albeit somewhat inelegant, method for dealing with real world uncertainties. However, the method must be used with care. Consider, for example, an active sonar that attempts to detect targets by emitting a sequence of short pulses, each of which might be reflected from a target in sufficient strength to be received. If $e = -3$ db and $\sigma = 6$ db, the probability of detection is $\Phi(-.5) = .31$ for any given pulse. The speed of sound in seawater is about 1500 m/sec, so a sonar with maximum range 6000 m would emit pulses every 2×6000 m/(1500 m/sec) = 8 sec; more closely spaced pulses would result in range ambiguities. In one minute, there would therefore be about 7 pulses emitted. If all 7 pulses were statistically independent, the probability that all 7 would miss the target would be $(.69)^7 = .07$, with a resultant probability of detection of .93. However, the assumption of independence is vital, and should not be made casually. Suppose, for example, that σ accounts primarily for uncertainty about target strength. While target strength might vary substantially over a large population of targets, there is no reason to expect the strength of a given target to vary much over a one minute period. If the first pulse misses, it might be explained by a low target strength, and low target strength implies that succeeding pulses are also likely to miss. In other words, successive pulses might not be statistically independent, and the probability of detection in the seven pulse example might be only a little larger than the probability of detection with a single pulse, rather than as large as .97.

The problem is even more severe with a passive sensor, since there is no obvious pacing mechanism analogous to the active pulse train. Naive methods for dealing with it generally produce detection probabilities that are optimistically high. The simplest of these would be to assume that all "looks" are independent, and that the interval Δ between looks has nothing to do with the detection process—perhaps Δ might be the length of the time step in a Monte Carlo simulation. If Δ is an arbitrary small number, then detection probabilities will be too high.

On the other hand, if Δ is regarded as a parameter that, like σ, is a measurable characteristic of the detection process, then the resulting passive detection model has some hope of producing accurate predictions. This "Fixed Scan" model is also attractive analytically, since there is a simple formula for calculating the probability of detection over a time interval $[a, b]$. Let S be the set of scans within the interval, and let

$$p(t) \equiv \Phi\big(e(t)/\sigma\big) \qquad (3.2\text{-}1)$$

be the detection probability for a scan at time t, where now the signal excess $e(t)$ is acknowledged to depend on time. Then the cumulative detection probability over the interval is

$$\mathrm{CDP}(a,b) = 1 - \prod_{t \in S}\big(1 - p(t)\big). \qquad (3.2\text{-}2)$$

In other words, there will be a detection in $[a, b]$ unless detection fails at every one of the independent scans within the interval.

The Fixed Scan model suffers from depending on an arbitrarily selected origin of time. By changing the origin, the locations or even the number of scans in set S could change, and likewise $\mathrm{CDP}(a, b)$ as computed by (3.2-2). The Poisson Scan model fixes this defect by assuming that scan opportunities come in a Poisson process with rate λ, rather than on a fixed schedule. The probability that a small time interval of length (dt) contains a successful scan at about time t is then $(\lambda\, dt)p(t)$, which is to say that $\lambda\, p(t)$ is the "detection rate" of Chapter 2. The cumulative detection probability over the interval $[a, b]$ is then

$$\mathrm{CDP}(a,b) = 1 - \exp\left(-\lambda\int_{a}^{b} p(t)\,dt\right). \qquad (3.2\text{-}3)$$

Formula (3.2-3) is more difficult to evaluate than (3.2-2), since an integral is required. However, in most cases the computational effort required will be trivial compared to the effort required to determine signal excess $e(t)$ over the interval $[a, b]$. For passive sensors, at least, the Poisson Scan model is therefore an improvement on the Fixed Scan model.

Unfortunately, *all* scan models suffer from the defect of permitting detections only at certain specific times. If signal excess rises to a large value, but only briefly, then (3.2-2) and (3.2-3) may both be small because the peak may occur between scan times. This is exactly what might happen when a submarine passes quickly through a strong but narrow convergence zone, or when a diesel submarine briefly surfaces to charge its batteries. To fix this defect, one must acknowledge that signal excess $E(t)$ is defined at all times, and that detection occurs within $[a, b]$ if the stochastic process $E(t)$ is *ever* positive within the interval. Since $E(t)$ is the difference between a predictable part $e(t)$ and an error part $X(t)$, the way in which $X(t)$ fluctuates with time must be quantified.

The simplest assumption about $X(t)$ is that it is unknown but constant over the interval $[a, b]$, in which case $E(t)$ will exceed zero somewhere in $[a, b]$ if and only if $E(t^*) > 0$, where t^* is the time in $[a, b]$ for which the predictable part $e(t)$ is maximal. Since $P(E(t^*) > 0) = p(t^*)$,

$$CDP(a, b) = p(t^*).\qquad(3.2\text{-}4)$$

In effect there is only one "scan" per interval, but that scan is evaluated at the most favorable point. Call this the Constant model.

The Constant model might be reasonable for short intervals $[a, b]$, but the assumption that $X(t)$ never changes is unduly pessimistic for long intervals. If $X(t)$ is instead hypothesized to change levels at times of a Poisson process with rate λ, then the resulting model is Kettelle's (λ, σ) model. The (λ, σ) model must be distinguished from the Poisson Scan model in spite of sharing the same parameter names; detection is possible at *any* time in the (λ, σ) model, rather than only at scan times. There is a simple formula for $CDP(a, b)$ only in the unimodal case where $e(t)$ has at most one local maximum within the interval (a, b). The simplest way of deriving this unimodal formula for the (λ, σ) model is to let time unfold both forwards and backwards from the maximal point t^*. Specifically, imagine determining $X(t)$ as follows:

1) At time t^*, let $X(t^*)$ be normal with mean zero and variance σ^2 (the $\otimes$ in Figure 3-6).

2) Proceed backwards in time, letting T_i be the Poisson times at which $X(t)$ changes level. At each such time, $X(t)$ jumps to a new, independently selected normal level (the O's in Figure 3-6).

3) Similarly to step 2, $X(t)$ is determined forwards in time from t^* by changing it at the times of a Poisson process.

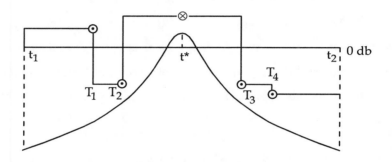

ILLUSTRATING NO DETECTION IN THE $(\lambda\text{-}\sigma)$ MODEL

The stochastic process $X(t)$ constructed in steps 1-3 is at all times normal, and is constant except at the jump times T_i. Furthermore, at each jump time the forward part is independent of the backward part. This method of constructing $X(t)$ makes it clear that $X(t)$ will lie entirely above $e(t)$ if and only if the single $\otimes$ and all of the O's lie above $e(t)$. The probability of the former is $1 - p(t^*)$, as in the Constant model. The probability of the latter is $\exp\left(-\lambda\int_a^b p(t)\,dt\right)$, as in the Poisson Scan model.

Therefore, since the events are independent,

$$\text{CDP}(a,b) = 1 - \left(1 - p(t^*)\right)\exp\left(-\lambda\int_a^b p(t)\,dt\right). \tag{3.2-5}$$

Given the same parameters, the $(\lambda\text{-}\sigma)$ model is more optimistic than either the Constant model (where detection is possible only at t^*) or the Poisson Scan model (where detection is possible at the Poisson times, but not at t^*).

The $(\lambda\text{-}\sigma)$ model is widely used in passive sonar modeling, particularly in tactical decision aids where there is the problem of evaluating $\text{CDP}(a, b)$ for thousands of hypothetical target tracks and for time intervals. There has consequently been some experimental work in the passive sonar context; Wagner [5] summarizes this work and gives approximate values $\lambda = 2/\text{hour}$ and $\sigma = 9$ db for passive sonar detections.

This wide use of the $(\lambda\text{-}\sigma)$ model is in spite of two inconvenient properties. The first has already been mentioned—except in the unimodal case, there is no simple formula for CDP (but see ref [1]). The second is that detections are not independent in nonoverlapping intervals; if $Q(a)$ is the probability of no detection up to time a, then it is not true that $Q(b) = Q(a)(1 - \text{CDP}(a, b))$. This makes it hard to apply Bayes Theorem, the usual method of updating probabilities to account for the passage of time.

It is disappointing that no cumulative detection probability model is both realistic and analytically convenient. Every model examined so far has liabilities as well as virtues, and all have been employed after due consideration at one time or another. The best model to use must depend on sensors and circumstances.

The reader may feel that Pandora's box has been opened in attempting to improve on the idea that detection will occur if and only if e is positive (the definite range law). It turns out that one usually cannot think of signal-to-noise ratio as being a random variable without being forced to think of it as a stochastic process, with all the mathematical complications that ensue. The effort is not without benefit, since the stochastic models fit reality better than the definite range law. Nonetheless, there are some arguments in favor of retreat. One is that the definite range law is easy to deal with, both conceptually and computationally, and therefore ought to be abandoned only in the face of massive evidence against it. Another is that e is often so sensitive to the range between searcher and target that the detection probability, however computed, is either very close to zero or very close to 1, in which case the definite range law is as good as any. See references [3, 4].

3.3 Radar Models

Radar systems are usually active, relying on the reflection of energy from the target. Pulse rates are much higher than in sonar because the speed of light in air (about 3×10^8 meters/second) is so much larger than the speed of sound in water (about 1.5×10^3 meters/second), and also because of the much higher frequencies involved. Although variations in the index of refraction near the earth's surface can cause anomalous propagation, for the most part the atmosphere is a more predictable environment for radar than is the ocean for sonar. The case for using cookie-cutter detection models is therefore probably better for radar than for sonar.

For active radar, errors in predicting signal excess are largely errors in predicting the "target strength", a term that represents the ability of the target to reflect energy back towards the transmitter. It is not unusual for this term to fluctuate by 20 db or more, depending on the aspect from which the target is viewed. Radar fluctuation theory therefore concentrates on this term. Most radar textbooks (e.g., [2]) will provide a good review under the index "Swerling".

CHAPTER 3. Exercises

1. To the extent that the ocean or atmosphere can be thought of as a homogeneous medium with no absorption or reflection, sonar or radar waves decrease in intensity at range r from the source according to the factor $1/r^2$. This is called spherical spreading; the amount of power per unit area (intensity) must be proportional to $1/r^2$ because the area of a sphere at range r is proportional to r^2 and power is conserved. For a passive system, this means that e has the form $e_1 - 20 \log_{10} r$, where e_1 incorporates all factors not related to range and r is measured in meters. Since the waves must travel out, be reflected, and travel back in an active system, the corresponding formula in an active system is $e_1 - 40 \log r$.

   a) Suppose $e_1 = 100$ db in a passive system. At what range would the signal excess e be zero? Note that the probability of detection at this range is .5, regardless of σ. If $\sigma = 6$ db, what would be the probability of detection at one-half this range? Same question at double the range?

   b) Suppose $e_1 = 160$ db in an active system. At what range would the signal excess e be zero? If $\sigma = 6$ db, what would the probability of detection be at one-half this range? Same question at double the range?

   c) On the basis of your computations in a) and b), would you say that the definite range law better approximates an active or a passive system?

   ANSWER: a) 100,000 meters, $\Phi(1) = .84$, $\Phi(-1) = .16$

                b) 10,000 meters, $\Phi(2) = .98$, $\Phi(-2) = .02$

                c) active.

2. $\Phi(e(t)/\sigma)$ is shown over a 6-hour period in the graph below. Let A be the event there is a detection somewhere in the interval $[-3, -1]$, and B be the event there is a detection somewhere in the interval $[-1, 3]$. What are $P(A)$, $P(B)$, $P(A \text{ or } B)$, and are A and B independent events, for the four CDP models specified below?

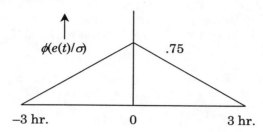

a) The Fixed Scan model with $\Delta = 2$ hours and with one end point at the origin.

b) The Poisson Scan model with $\lambda = 1/(3 \text{ hours})$.

c) The Constant model.

d) The $(\lambda$-$\sigma)$ model with $\lambda = 1/(3 \text{ hours})$.

ANSWER: a)   .25, .81, .86, yes

b)   .15, .44, .53, yes

c)   .5, .75, .75, no

d)   .58, .86, .88, no

3. Where does the argument justifying Formula 3.1-6 break down if $e(t)$ is not unimodal? Draw a picture similar to Figure 3-6 to illustrate the difficulty.

REFERENCES

[1]   Belkin, B. 1971. First passage to a general threshold for a process corresponding to sampling at poisson times. *J. Appl. Probab.* **8** 573–588.

[2]   Skolnik, M. 1980. *Introduction to Radar Systems*. McGraw-Hill.

[3]   Loane, E. P., H. R. Richardson, E. S. Boylan. 1969. Theory of cumulative detection probability. Daniel H. Wagner, Associates report to the Naval Underwater Sound Laboratory DOC No. AD 615497.

[4]   McCabe, B. J. 1974. Comparison of stochastic processes used in sonar detection models. *Naval Res. Logist. Quart.* **21** 673–682.

[5]   Wagner, D. 1989. Naval tactical decision aids. Naval Postgraduate School Report NPSOR-90-01.

4. LATERAL RANGE CURVES/SWEEPWIDTH

4.1 Lateral Range Curves

The models of detection introduced in Chapter 3 are complex, and the real world even more so. The ocean in particular is notoriously variable in ways not easily described. It is therefore tempting to describe search capability through experiments where a searcher performs a specified maneuver in an attempt at detection, rather than by trying to discover fundamental parameters of the environment and then reasoning deductively. In theory one repeats the experiment often enough to establish detection probability in the conditions under which the experiment is performed. This is the idea behind lateral range curves.

In a lateral range experiment, the track of the searcher relative to the target is a straight line, with the lateral range being the distance between the line and the target at the point of closest approach. The distance is usually considered to be signed, with the situation illustrated in the left of Figure 4-2 being a positive lateral range. In theory the experimenter observes only whether detection occurs somewhere on the line, ignoring the true range at which it occurs. By performing sufficiently many independent trials, the probability of detection $p(x)$ can be established for encounters that have lateral range x. The graph of this function is the lateral range curve [2], an example of which is shown on the right of Figure 4-2. The example makes the point that lateral range curves are not necessarily symmetric, even though that is usually the case. A "cookie-cutter" sensor detects targets if and only if the target range is smaller than R; such a sensor has a lateral range curve that is 1 if $|x| \leq R$, or otherwise zero.

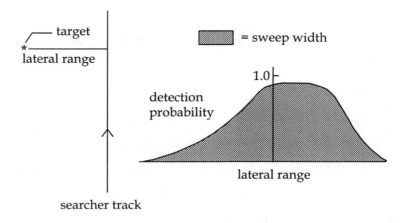

target

lateral range

= sweep width

1.0

detection
probability

lateral range

searcher track

ILLUSTRATING LATERAL RANGE CURVES AND SWEEPWIDTH

At this point the reader may wish to review the developments in Section 2.4 leading up to Formula 2.4-3, which is an analytic expression for the lateral range curve of an inverse cube law sensor.

It should be apparent that actually proceeding in the manner sketched above would be extremely expensive. Measuring even a single probability is a nontrivial undertaking, particularly if one is required to assure that the trials are independent, and a lateral range curve consists of many such probability measurements. Additionally, the number of curves required may be large because of the need to make measurements in a variety of environments. For example, sonar detection ranges are strongly affected by geographic location and season. In practice, a variety of techniques are employed to wring as much information as possible out of measured data.

In situations where it is clear on physical grounds that the lateral range curve must be symmetric and unimodal, it may be useful to employ the parametric class of lateral range curves

$$p(x) = 1 - \exp\left(-\left|\frac{x_0}{x}\right|^b\right); \quad -\infty < x < \infty, \qquad (4.1\text{-}1)$$

where x_0 is a scaling and b a shape parameter. The class includes both the definite range law ($b = \infty$) and the inverse cube law ($b = 2$) as special cases, and has convenient analytic properties. $p(x)$ is shown in Figure 4-3 as a function of the normalized lateral range x/x_0.

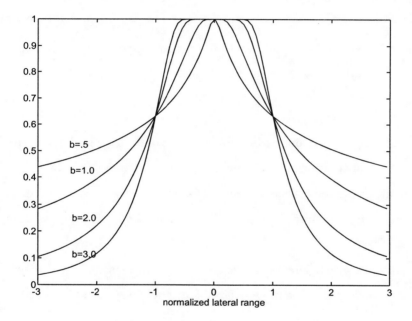

A PARAMETRIC CLASS OF LATERAL RANGE CURVES

Iida [1] derives (4.1-1) from the assumption that the detection rate function of Chapter 2 is proportional to $r^{-(b+1)}$, with r being range. Thus 4.1-1 is the lateral range curve for the "inverse $b + 1$ law". For $b > 1$, the sweepwidth W defined in the next section is

$$W = 2x_0\,\Gamma(1 - 1/b), \qquad\qquad (4.1\text{-}2)$$

where Γ is the Gamma function. The sweepwidth is infinite for $b \le 1$. The parameters b and x_0 can be estimated using the Maximum Likelihood Method (see Exercise 5).

An important use of lateral range curves is in investigating the effects of spacing in barriers or in sweeping an area. If x is the lateral range to one sensor and S is the spacing, then the lateral ranges to the other sensors are $x \pm S$, $x \pm 2S$, etc. Letting $\hat{p}(x)$ be the probability that at least one sensor detects the target, and assuming independence of the various detection events, we have

$$\hat{p}(x) = 1 - \prod_i \left(1 - p(x + iS)\right), \qquad\qquad (4.1\text{-}3)$$

where the product extends over whatever set of positive and negative values for i is appropriate. This will lead to a convenient product of exponentials for the class of curves 4.1-1. In the case of the inverse cube law and an infinite line of sensors, there is a closed form expression for $\hat{p}(x)$ (Section 2.4).

Lateral range curves can be traced back at least to World War II [2]. There is some discussion of associated statistical issues in Chapter 11.

4.2   Sweepwidth

Sweepwidth W is defined to be the area underneath the lateral range curve:

$$W = \int_{-\infty}^{\infty} p(x)dx. \qquad\qquad (4.2\text{-}1)$$

Note that W has units of length, and that the sweepwidth of a cookie cutter sensor with definite range R is $W = 2R$. W is the shaded area in Figure

4-2. Sweepwidth is a scalar measure of the search effectiveness of a sensor, and is thus relatively easy to tabulate. The National Search and Rescue Manual [3] gives sweepwidths for a variety of sensors and environments.

It is sometimes true that a sensor with sweepwidth W is "equivalent" to a cookie-cutter sensor with definite range $R = W/2$. Suppose that a sensor has a series of encounters with a target, each of which is characterized by a random lateral range with probability density function $f(x)$. Then the probability of detection in an encounter is $p_d = \int_{-\infty}^{\infty} p(x)f(x)dx$. If the lateral range is typically large compared to the sensor's detection capability, then it is reasonable to assume that $f(x)$ is approximately constant (call it f_0) over some large interval $[-L,L]$ that includes most of the area under $p(x)$. This would be the case, for example, if a searcher were searching at random for a target in a region whose dimensions were much larger than the sweepwidth. The probability of detection in an encounter is then approximately

$$p_d \cong \int_{-L}^{L} p(x)f(x)dx \cong f_0 \int_{-L}^{L} p(x)dx \cong f_0 W ,\qquad (4.2\text{-}2)$$

provided $f_0 W \ll 1$. If we wanted to determine the probability of detection over a specific period of time, we would have to deal with the frequency of encounters, the magnitude of f_0, etc., but the only point worth noting here is that all lateral range curves with the same sweepwidth will give the same answer. In particular, there is no harm in conceptually replacing the actual sensor with a cookie-cutter sensor in problems where the above assumptions are reasonable.

There are, of course, problems where the cookie-cutter equivalence idea is not valid. For example, if a region is searched exhaustively with a cookie-cutter sensor, then the probability of detection is 1, but if a searcher follows the same path with an inverse cube law sensor having the same sweepwidth, the probability of detection is only .79 (see Figure 2-4). Also, if $b < 1$ in 4.1-1, then the sweepwidth is infinite. This does not mean that such a sensor is absurd, but it does mean that it is not equivalent to a cookie cutter sensor with the same sweepwidth.

In summary, the cookie-cutter equivalence idea is valid as long as the detection process consists of a series of encounters each of which has an independently random closest point of approach that is typically large compared to the sweepwidth. It is not valid in many situations where it would be very useful; specifically, in situations where it would be handy to use geometry to design a search pattern. Use of cookie-cutter equivalence in such situations will typically result in calculating a probability of detection that is too large.

4.3 RelMin, an Approximation Procedure for Crooked Paths

Even though a lateral range curve is an incomplete summary of a sensor, it sometimes happens that a lateral range curve is all that is available for analyzing a problem where the relative track between sensor and target is not a complete, straight line. An exact calculation of the detection probability is impossible, but an approximation is still desired. Procedure RelMin is a technique for approximating the detection probability, when the target is stationary, while the sensor moves over a continuous path that consists of a series of line segments.

Let the path consist of segments $1,...,n$, with $n \geq 1$ and segment i connecting point u_{i-1} to point u_i. Here u_i stands for (x_i, y_i), a point in two dimensions, with (x_0, y_0) being the start point. Each of the segments may or may not have an interior closest point of approach (CPA), by which is meant that there is a line connecting the target to the segment that meets it in an interior point at a right angle (several such interior points are indicated with arrows in Figure 4-8). If all of the segments are long and have interior CPAs, it would be reasonable to treat the segments as being independent and infinitely long. Procedure RelMin does this for such paths, but is also capable of estimating the detection probability for any path.

RelMin begins by constructing a set of relative minimum points for each path. Each segment with an interior CPA has a relative minimum at that point, which is included in the set. In addition, a segment's start point is included if

- the segment has no interior minumum;
- the start point is at least as close as the segment's end point; and,
- the start point is closer than the previous segment's end point (this last qualification is omitted for the first segment).

The end point of a segment is never counted, so there is at most one relative minimum per segment. Once the list of relative minimum points is generated, a detection probability for each point is calculated by evaluating the lateral range curve at the distance of the point from the target. A detection probability for the whole path is then determined by assuming segment independence. In principle, a different lateral range curve could be used for each segment, possibly because the searcher's speed differs among the segments.

It is conceivable that there will be no relative minima, in which case the detection probability will be zero. This will happen if each point is closer to the target than its predecessor.

Procedure RelMin has some desirable properties:

- The detection probability is easy to compute.
- Any path can be decomposed into independent subpaths without changing the detection probability.
- Any segment can be subdivided into subsegments without changing the detection probability.
- The right answer is obtained for a path consisting of a single, infinitely long line.

On the other hand, RelMin can also give some patently optimistic answers. On the left of Figure 4-8, a raster-type track has three relative minima in a short interval of time for the indicated target, with even the short segment being treated as if it were infinitely long. The right of Figure 4-8 shows how a basically circular path around the target can have a relative minimum for every segment. As the circular track is approximated more and more closely by increasing the number of segments, the cumulative detection probability approaches 1!

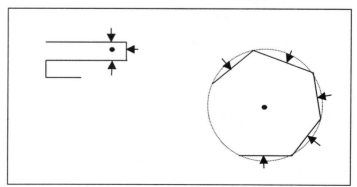

PATHS ILLUSTRATING PROBLEMS WITH THE RelMin PROCEDURE

No procedure can give accurate results for all paths, given only a lateral range curve. In specific circumstances, however, there may be better approximation procedures than RelMin. One such alternative procedure is sometimes used with "raster" paths that consist of alternate short and long segments, as in the left of Figure 4-8. The modification to RelMin is that short segments do not contribute relative minima. In essence, the path is approximated by arguing that the long segments are effectively infinite, and that the short segments contribute nothing to detection. Another alternative procedure would be to test only the closest of all the relative minima; i.e., the global CPA for the path.

Page "RelMin" of *Search4.xls* implements the RelMin procedure for the case of an inverse-cube law lateral range curve. When the lateral range curve is symmetric, the RelMin procedure can be implemented without taking any square roots, as in the Visual Basic subroutine Segment() that supports the calculations on that page.

CHAPTER 4: Exercises

1. Five sensors are located at positions 0, 10, 20, 30, and 40 on a line. Each has the lateral range curve $p(x) = 1 - \exp(-1/|x|)$. A target travels along the infinite line illustrated below. What is the probability that the target is detected by at least one of the sensors, assuming independence?

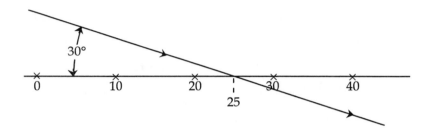

ANSWER: .682. You only need to use the exponential function once.

2. A searcher spends 10 hours randomly looking for a target in a square with side 20 miles. He travels at 10 miles/hr, and uses a sensor with lateral range curve $1 - \exp(-1/x^4)$, where x is in miles. What is the probability that he will detect the target? Hint: $\Gamma(3/4) = 1.225$.
ANSWER: From 4.1-2, $W = 2\Gamma(3/4) = 2.45$. This is much less than 20, so use Section 2.2 to obtain $1 - \exp(-245/400) = .46$.

3. If $p(x) = \exp(-x^2/2)$, what is W?
ANSWER: $W = 2.51$.

4. A vehicle carries three independent sensors. The ith sensor detects a target with probability β_i if the lateral range is less than the sensor's maximum range $.5\,M_i$, so the sweepwidth for sensor i is $W_i = \beta_i\,M_i$.

a) If $M_i = 2i$ and $\beta_i = .5$ for $i = 1, 2, 3$, sketch the joint lateral range curve for the three sensors and compute the joint sweepwidth.

b) If $M_1 < M_2 < M_3$, derive the formula $W_3 + W_2(1 - \beta_3) + W_1(1 - \beta_2)$ $(1 - \beta_3)$ for the joint sweepwidth.

ANSWER: In part a), the lateral range curve is a step function with sweepwidth 4.25. The three sensor formula is a special case of the n sensor formula $W_n + \sum_{j=1}^{n-1} W_j \prod_{k=j+1}^{n} (1 - \beta_k)$ given in reference [3] of Chapter 5.

5. A lateral range experiment is performed at lateral ranges -5, -4, ..., 4, 5, a total of 11 runs. One additional run is made at lateral range 5, making 12 runs in all. All runs result in detection except the runs at -5, -3, 3, and one of the runs at 5. Find Maximum Likelihood estimates of the parameters b and x_0 of Section 4.1, and the corresponding sweepwidth. Use sheet "LatRng" of *Search4.xls*. That sheet expects there to be 14 runs, but runs at lateral range zero that result in detection do not affect the computation, so they can be inserted as needed to make the total 14.

ANSWER: $x_0 = 3.01$, $b = 1.52$, $w = .96$.

6. Suppose that the range of a sensor is either 100 or 200 meters, depending on whether the target is wounded or not (wounded targets tend to lie down, so they can only be detected at close range). Suppose further that half of all targets are wounded.

a) Sketch the lateral range curve, and give the sweepwidth.

ANSWER: The sweepwidth is 150 meters.

b) If the searcher were to follow a crooked path, suggest an improvement to RelMin for calculating the cumulative detection probability in situations like this where the principal uncertainty is about the status of the target.

7. A searcher follows a crooked path that connects the five points (0,0), (1,1), (1,2), (3,1), and (3,0). A target is located at (2,1). The lateral range curve is inverse cube law with a sweepwidth of 2. Including all four segments of the searcher's path, what is the detection probability according to the RelMin procedure? Hint: Either make a sketch or use page "RelMin" of workbook *Search4.xls*.

ANSWER: .852.

REFERENCES

[1]   Iida, K. 1993. Inverse N^{th} power detection law for Washburn's lateral range curve. *J. Oper. Res. Soc. Japan* **36** 90–101.

[2]   Koopman, B. 1956. The theory of search (II). *Oper. Res.* **4** 503–531.

[3]   *National Search and Rescue Manual.* 1991. JOINT PUB 3-50 and 3-50.1, Joint Chiefs of Staff, Washington, D.C.

5. EFFORT DISTRIBUTION PROBLEMS/STATIONARY TARGETS

Suppose that the target is known to be in one of n not necessarily identical regions, with p_i being the probability that the target is in the ith region. In applications, the numbers p_i quantify the judgment of some expert or group of experts as to likelihood. Part of the reason why the correct region is unknown may be previous random motion on the part of the target, but the target is nonetheless supposed to be stationary (stay in one region) during the search. In any case, we take the distribution $p_1, \ldots, p_n$ to be given.

Figure 5-2 shows the initial distribution used in one application. The nuclear submarine USS *Scorpion* was lost in 1968, and a search was conducted for the remains. Multiple scenarios (collision with seamount, torpedo going active, etc.) were considered by experts for what might have happened to the boat, which explains the multi-peakedness of the distribution. Each of the 20 × 16 regions in Figure 5-2 is 1 mile in the latitude direction and .84 miles in the longitude direction, and the view is from the southeast. The region with the largest peak has a probability of 12.5%. After several months of searching with sonar in deep water, the remains of *Scorpion* were eventually found at the base of that peak [3]. Throughout the search, decisions constantly had to be made about how subsequent effort should be distributed over the regions. The problem considered in this chapter can be thought of as an extreme case where the available effort is allocated all at once.

The distribution of effort (DOE) problem is to divide a total amount of time t into an amount of time t_i for each region in such a manner as to maximize the probability of detection. If the dimension of each region is large compared to the sweepwidth of the sensor in that region, it may be reasonable to suppose that the random search formula holds in each region. In that case, the probability of detecting the target, <u>given</u> that it is actually in region i, is $1 - \exp(-t_i/\tau_i)$, where $\tau_i = A_i/V_i W_i$ is the mean time to detection in region i (Section 2.2). The unconditional probability of detection is then $p = \sum_{i=1}^{n} p_i \left(1 - \exp(-t_i/\tau_i)\right)$, and the object is to maximize p subject to $t_i \geq 0$ and $\sum_{i=1}^{n} t_i \leq t$. This is the problem considered in Sections 5.1, 5.2, and 5.3.

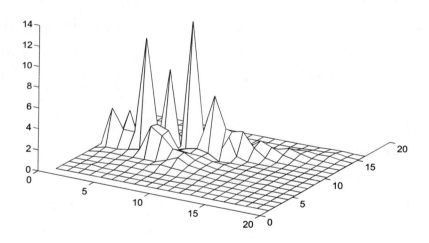

INITIAL DISTRIBUTION FOR USS *SCORPION*

The problem of maximizing p is a constrained optimization problem, so it cannot be solved by equating derivatives with respect to t_i to zero. However, it can be solved by any general purpose constrained optimizer. Sheet "Effort(2)" of *Search4.xls* is set up to do this for a problem with 10 cells, using Excel's Solver optimizer. More efficient methods will exploit the analytic structure of the problem. One such method uses Everett's Theorem to deal with this constraint.

5.1. Everett's Theorem

Theorem: Let $f(x)$ and $g(x)$ be two scalar functions defined on any set whatever, and suppose that the Lagrangian function $L(x) \equiv f(x) - \lambda g(x)$ has a maximum at x^*, where $\lambda \geq 0$. Then the maximum of $f(x)$, subject to $g(x) \leq g(x^*)$, is $f(x^*)$.

Proof: [1] The proof is by contradiction. Suppose $f(x') > f(x^*)$ and $g(x') \leq g(x^*)$. Then $f(x') - \lambda g(x') > f(x^*) - \lambda g(x^*)$, which contradicts the hypothesis that x^* maximizes $L(x)$. Q.E.D.

In practice, one uses Everett's Theorem on problems where maximization of the Lagrangian is so simple that one does not mind the bother of having to find the Lagrange multiplier λ for which $g(x^*)$ is equal to some desired figure. One can think of $g(x)$ as a resource and λ as the price of the resource. If λ is too high, less resource than is actually available will be consumed, or else too much will be consumed if λ is too low. If exactly the right value for λ can be found, then Everett's Theorem states that a constrained optimization problem has been solved. If Everett's Theorem were false, Economics would have to be heavily revised.

Since we only have one resource (time) in mind, we have not proved the more general version of Everett's Theorem where there are multiple resources and Lagrange multipliers.

5.2.   The General Case

To apply Everett's Theorem to the problem posed earlier, let $\underline{x}$ be the non-negative vector $(t_1, \ldots, t_n)$, $f(\underline{x}) = \sum_{i=1}^{n} p_i\left(1 - \exp(-t_i/\tau_i)\right)$, and $g(\underline{x}) = \sum_{i=1}^{n} t_i$. The Lagrangian function $L(\underline{x})$ is then $\sum_{i=1}^{n} f_i(t_i)$, where

$f_i(t_i) = p_i(1 - \exp(-t_i/\tau_i)) - \lambda t_i$. For each i, $f_i(t_i)$ is to be maximized subject to $t_i \geq 0$. The advantage of the Lagrangian approach is that each index i can be optimized without reference to the others. By equating the derivative of $f_i(t_i)$ to 0, we find $t_i = \tau_i \ln(p_i/\lambda\tau_i)$. Since $f_i(t_i)$ is a concave function, this is optimal as long as it is positive; otherwise, we should set $t_i = 0$. Thus, the optimal solution is

$$\begin{cases} \text{if } \lambda\tau_i \leq p_i, t_i = \tau_i \ln(p_i/\lambda\tau_i) \ \text{ and } \ f_i(t_i) = p_i - \lambda\tau_i \\ \text{if } \lambda\tau_i \geq p_i, t_i = 0 \ \text{ and } \ f_i(t_i) = 0. \end{cases} \qquad (5.2\text{-}1)$$

The only remaining problem is to find the value of λ for which $\sum_{i=1}^{n} t_i \leq t$. This can be done by trial and error, increasing λ if $\sum_{i=1}^{n} t_i$ is too large, etc. One method of doing this is shown in the flow diagram below, where <u>both</u> sums are over the set of subscripts I for which $t_i > 0$:

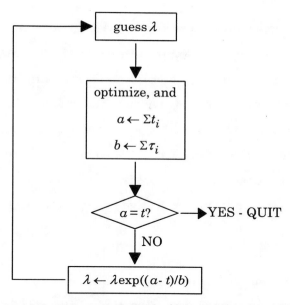

FLOW DIAGRAM FOR OPTIMAL DISTRIBUTION OF EFFORT

Notice that the last step in Figure 5-5 has the effect of increasing λ if too much time is used ($a > t$) or decreasing λ otherwise. The method of doing this has the important virtue that the number of passes around the loop will not exceed $n + 2$ as long as the initial guess at λ is small enough that at least one positive t_i results [5]. Table 5-5 shows the sequence of computations if $n = 10$, $t = 5$, $p_i = .1$, and $\tau_i = i$. The initial (bad) guess for λ is .0001.

λ	t_1	t_2	t_3	t_4	t_5	t_6	t_7	t_8	t_9	t_{10}	a	b
.0001	6.9	12.4	17.4	22.1	26.5	30.7	34.7	38.6	42.4	46.1	278	55
.0143	2.0	2.5	2.6	2.2	1.7	.9	.01	0	0	0	11.9	28
.0183	1.7	2.0	1.8	1.3	.5	0	0	0	0	0	7.3	15
.0213	1.6	1.7	1.4	.6	0	0	0	0	0	0	5.3	10
.0218	1.5	1.7	1.3	.5	0	0	0	0	0	0	5.0	10

ILLUSTRATION OF CONVERGENCE IN FIVE STEPS

From 5.2-1, the probability of detection in the last line of Table 5-5 is $4(.1) - \lambda(1 + 2 + 3 + 4) = .182$. It is interesting that Region 2 has more effort (1.7) placed in it than any other region. τ_5 is so large that it is not worthwhile to allocate any effort to region 5, and τ_1 is so small that a very high probability of detection can be achieved with only a small amount of effort; the region with the most effort allocated has a mean time to detection that is neither very large nor very small. Note that the procedure provides an automatic sensitivity analysis, since the optimal distribution of effort when $t = 5.3$, 7.3, 11.9, and 278, as well as when $t = 5$, is produced.

In practice, some provision must be made for the possibility that the initial guess at λ is so large that no effort at all is allocated, in which case $a = b = 0$. A simple remedy is to select the initial λ so that $\lambda < p_i/\tau_i$ for some i. Then from 5.2-1, $t_i > 0$.

Sheet "Effort" of *Search4.xls* is set up to perform one iteration of this procedure, which the user can repeat if desired. An alternative optimization approach is the "Charnes-Cooper" algorithm [4].

5.3   Search of a Normal Prior

It often happens that the distribution of the target's position is a bivariate normal probability density function (p.d.f.) $f(x,y)$ with standard deviations σ_X and σ_Y; that is,

$$f(x,y) = \exp\left[-\frac{1}{2}\left((x/\sigma_X)^2 + (y/\sigma_Y)^2\right)\right]\Big/(2\pi\sigma_X\sigma_Y).$$

Assuming that the sweepwidth W is such that $\sigma_X >> W$ and $\sigma_Y >> W$, it will be possible to divide the plane up into regions or cells such that

a) the p.d.f. is nearly constant within each cell; and

b) W is small with respect to the cell dimension.

The general procedure of Section 5.2 could then be carried out, with p_i being the amount of probability in cell i. The purpose of this section is to make an analytical approximation to the probability of detection that would be obtained in that case. To simplify calculations, assume $\sigma_X = \sigma_Y = \sigma$, but all results remain correct if $\sqrt{\sigma_X \sigma_Y}$ is substituted for σ.

Define $d(x,y)$ to be the amount of time per unit area spent searching in the vicinity of the point (x,y), and let A_i be the area of the cell that includes (x,y). Then the amount of time t_i spent searching in cell i is $d(x,y)A_i$. If V and W are the speed and sweepwidth of the searcher (assumed to be the same in all cells), then $VWt_i/A_i = VWd(x,y)$, and the probability of detecting the target given that it is located at (x,y) is $1 - \exp(-VWd(x,y))$, as in Section 2.2. Averaging over (x,y), we obtain the probability of detection p:

$$p = \int\int f(x,y)\left[1 - \exp(-VWd(x,y))\right]dxdy. \qquad (5.3\text{-}1)$$

In attempting to maximize p, we must choose $d(x,y)$ such that $\int\int d(x,y)\,dxdy = t$ and $d(x,y) \geq 0$. This is a constrained optimization problem, to which we apply Everett's Theorem (Section 5.1). It is convenient in this case to let

$$\lambda = VW \exp\left(-\frac{r_0^2}{2\sigma^2}\right)\Big/2\pi\sigma^2,$$

where r_0 is as yet unspecified. The Lagrangian function is then:

$$L(d) = \frac{1}{2\pi\sigma^2}\int\int\left[\exp\left(-\frac{x^2+y^2}{2\sigma^2}\right)\left[1 - \exp(-VWd(x,y))\right]\right.$$

$$\left. -VW \exp\left(-\frac{r_0^2}{2\sigma^2}\right)d(x,y)\right]dxdy. \qquad (5.3\text{-}2)$$

The Lagrangian $L(d)$ will be maximized if $d(x,y)$ maximizes the integrand at every point (x,y). As in Section 5.2, we can solve this problem by equating the derivative of the integrand with respect to $d(x,y)$ to zero, and then checking to see that the result is positive. The optimal function $d(x,y)$ is:

$$d(x,y) = \begin{cases} \dfrac{r_0^2 - x^2 - y^2}{2VW\sigma^2} & \text{for } x^2 + y^2 \leq r_0^2 \\ 0 & \text{otherwise.} \end{cases} \tag{5.3-3}$$

To discover the proper value of r_0, write the constraint in polar coordinates:

$$\iint d(x,y)\,dx\,dy = t,$$

so

$$\int_0^{2\pi} \int_0^{r_0} \left(\frac{r_0^2 - r^2}{2VW\sigma^2} \right) r\,dr\,d\theta = t,$$

or

$$\left(\frac{2\pi}{2VW\sigma^2} \right)\left(\frac{r_0^4}{2} - \frac{r_0^4}{4} \right) = t.$$

Therefore r_0, which turns out to be the maximum range at which search is carried out, is given by

$$r_0 = \sigma(8z)^{\frac{1}{4}}, \tag{5.3-4}$$

where

$$z = VWt/(2\pi\sigma^2).^* \tag{5.3-5}$$

---

* In the elliptical case, $d(x,y) = \left(r_0^2/\sigma_X\sigma_Y - x^2/\sigma_X^2 - y^2/\sigma_Y^2 \right)\big/2VW$ and $z = VWt/(2\pi\sigma_X\sigma_Y)$.

We now know the optimal function $d(x,y)$. The probability of detection is zero if the target is outside a circle of radius r_0, so, writing 5.3-1 in polar coordinates,

$$p = \frac{1}{2\pi\sigma^2} \int_0^{2\pi} \int_0^{r_0} \exp\left(-\frac{r^2}{2\sigma^2}\right)\left(1 - \exp\left(-\frac{r_0^2 - r^2}{2\sigma^2}\right)\right) r\,dr\,d\theta$$

$$= \frac{1}{\sigma^2} \int_0^{r_0} \left[\left[\exp\left(-\frac{r^2}{2\sigma^2}\right)\right] - \left[\exp\left(-\frac{r_0^2}{\sigma^2}\right)\right]\right] r\,dr$$

$$= \left[1 - \exp\left(-\frac{r_0^2}{2\sigma^2}\right)\right] - \left[\frac{r_0^2}{2\sigma^2}\exp\left(-\frac{r_0^2}{2\sigma^2}\right)\right].$$

Since $r_0^2/(2\sigma^2) = \sqrt{2z}$, this reduces to

$$p = 1 - \left(1 + \sqrt{2z}\right)\exp\left(-\sqrt{2z}\right). \tag{5.3-6}$$

Formula 5.3-6 shows how detection probability depends on time available when the search effort is locally random but nonetheless optimally distributed over the plane (the SOLR curve in Figure 5-10). The optimal distribution of effort is zero outside a circle of radius r_0, becoming more intense at points near the origin in the manner of 5.3-3. The cumulative version of 5.3-3 is sometimes more useful as a tool for designing approximately optimal searches. Let $F(u)$ be the fraction of total search effort spent within a distance ur_0 of the origin, so that $F(1) = 1$. Then, from 5.3-3, with $v = r/r_0$,

$$F(u) = \frac{1}{2VWt\sigma^2} \int_0^{2\pi} \int_0^{ur_0} \left(r_0^2 - r^2\right) r\,dr\,d\theta$$

$$F(u) = (\text{const.})\int_0^u \left(1 - v^2\right)v\,dv \tag{5.3-7}$$

$$F(u) = 2u^2 - u^4, \quad \text{since } F(1) = 1.$$

For example, the searcher should spend 7/16 of his time inside a circle of radius $r_0/2$, whereas he would spend only 1/4 of his time there if his effort were spread uniformly over the circle. If actually there is a large number n of discrete "looks", each of which covers an area "a", then one can simply replace VWt by na in the definition of z. $F(u)$ is then the fraction of looks within ur_0 of the origin.

The search analyzed above might be called strategically optimal but locally random (SOLR). It is interesting to compare Formula 5.3-6 with the equivalent result for a search that is optimal both locally and strategically, an exhaustive search. The region searched exhaustively should be a circle with area VWt, and the probability of detection is simply the probability that the target lies within the circle. The radius of the circle is $\rho = \sqrt{VWt/\pi}$, so

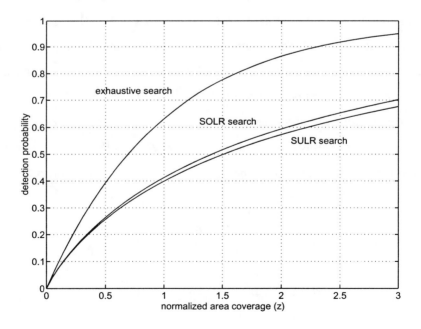

THREE TYPES OF SEARCH ON A NORMAL DENSITY

$$p = \frac{1}{2\pi\sigma^2} \int_0^\rho \exp\left(-\frac{r^2}{2\sigma^2}\right) r\,dr\,d\theta$$

$$= 1 - \exp\left(-\frac{\rho^2}{2\sigma^2}\right) = 1 - \exp(-z), \tag{5.3-8}$$

where z is as defined in 5.3-5. This formula is shown in Figure 5-10 as the "exhaustive search" curve. Naturally, it gives a larger detection probability than 5.3-6.

In some circumstances, it may be too much trouble to carry out a SOLR search because of the need in that type of search to spend differing amounts of time in different places. A simpler search would be to simply pick a circle and search uniformly at random within the circle. If the circle is picked to maximize the detection probability, this is the "strategically uniform locally random" (SULR) search. Let ρ be the radius of the circle. The probability that the target is inside the circle is $1 - \exp\left[-\left(\rho^2/2\sigma^2\right)\right]$.

Since density of searching effort within the circle is $t/(\pi\rho^2)$, the probability of detection <u>given</u> that the target is within the circle is $1 - \exp(-VWt/(\pi\rho^2))$. The circle radius ρ should therefore be chosen to maximize the product

$$\left[1 - \exp\left(-\frac{\rho^2}{2\sigma^2}\right)\right]\left[1 - \exp\left(-\frac{VWt}{\pi\rho^2}\right)\right].$$

It is left as an exercise to show that the optimal value of $\rho^2/(2\sigma^2)$ is $\sqrt{z}$, and that the resulting detection probability for SULR search is

$$p = [1 - \exp(-\sqrt{z})]^2. \tag{5.3-9}$$

This is also shown in Figure 5-10. It is of course the lowest of the three curves, but note that 5.3-9 differs very little from 5.3-6. If a search is to be locally random, it is evidently not vital that it be strategically optimal.

Each of the three curves in Figure 5-10 has a mean time to detection $E(T)$ associated with it, where T is the random time to detection of a searcher who continues to search until he finds the target. Utilizing Formula 2.1-5, and letting $\tau = 2\pi\sigma^2/VW$, the mean times can be shown to be τ, 3τ, and 3.5τ in the cases of exhaustive, SOLR, and SULR searches.

Sheet "SULR_SOLR" of *Search4.xls* is set up to compare the results of a simulation with Formulas (5.3-6) and (5.3-9). It is assumed on that sheet that search is conducted in a sequence of n looks, with n and the look radius R being input. The total amount of search effort is then $n\pi R^2$ instead of VWt, but otherwise the problem formulation is the same. Since each of the looks is independently located, the search pattern will look like a random fall of confetti as long as n is large. Problems of this kind arise in designing cluster weapons, as well as in search.

5.4. Myopic Search with Discrete Looks

As in Section 5.2, let p_i represent the probability that the target is in the ith region or "cell". However, suppose now that effort is measured in "looks", rather than continuously. There are several motivations for doing this, among which are:

a) It may be necessary to measure time in multiples of some fundamental interval that cannot be subdivided, in which case the fundamental interval is a "look".

b) A look may correspond to completion of a particular search pattern.

c) The optimal method of allocating looks to cells is particularly simple if the looks are allocated sequentially, as we shall see.

Assume that successive looks in the ith cell each have probability q_i of not detecting the target, independent of all other looks. If k_i is the number of looks in the ith cell, then the probability of detection is

$p = \sum_{i=1}^{n} p_i\left(1 - q_i^{k_i}\right)$, and the object is to maximize p subject to $k_1 \geq 0$ and a

constraint on $\sum_{i=1}^{n} k_i$, where n is the number of cells. Lagrangian methods

can be applied to the solution of this problem, just as in the continuous case. However, it is instructive to consider an inductive technique that depends in an essential way on the discrete nature of the looks.

Suppose that the allocation problem for k looks has somehow been solved, with the optimal allocation being $k_1, ..., k_n$, and that the problem is to allocate $k + 1$ looks. One method of doing this would be to add the $k + 1$st look to the cell with the highest incremental payoff: in the ith cell, this incremental payoff is

$$p_i\left(1 - q_i^{k_i+1}\right) - p_i\left(1 - q_i^{k_i}\right) = p_i(1 - q_i)q_i^{k_i} .$$

The procedure of allocating every look in this manner is called the "greedy algorithm"—looks are allocated one at a time with each look going to the cell where it will do the most good, starting with $k = 0$. The greedy algorithm will produce optimal allocations in this problem because $p_i\left(1 - q_i^{k_i}\right)$ is a concave function of k_i.[*]

Table 5-14 shows the operation of the algorithm for the case $n = 3$, $(p_1, p_2, p_3) = (.5, .4, .1)$, and $(q_1, q_2, q_3) = (.5, .8, 0)$.

_____

[*] But the greedy algorithm does not work in general. Given five dollars and the opportunity to buy cigars at one dollar each or else a box of 10 cigars for five dollars, the algorithm would buy five cigars, one at a time.

k	$p_1(1-q_1)q_1^{k_1}$	$p_2(1-q_2)q_2^{k_2}$	$p_3(1-q_3)q_3^{k_3}$	search cell
0	.25	.08	.1	1
1	.125	.08	.1	1
2	.0625	.08	.1	3
3	.0625	.08	0	2
4	.0625	.064	0	2
5	.0625	.0512	0	1
6				

AN OPTIMAL SEQUENCE OF DISCRETE LOOKS

The arithmetic is quite simple. The first three numbers (.25, .08, .1) are calculated directly from (p_1, p_2, p_3) and (q_1, q_2, q_3). The largest of these is the first, so the first look goes in cell 1, and in general one always looks in the cell with the largest number. Then the next line is obtained by multiplying the number in the searched cell by the relevant q_i, etc. The amount of computation required is evidently proportional to the largest number of looks considered.

If the object in the above example is to maximize the probability of detection after six looks, then the only important thing is that there be three looks in the first cell, two looks in the second, and one in the third. The looks do not have to be in the sequence 1, 1, 3, 2, 2, 1. This observation could be important if there were a penalty of some sort for moving from cell to cell. However, a searcher who wants to minimize the average number of looks required to find the target should make the looks in the same order in which they are computed. In fact, making the looks in the order in which they are computed is called a uniformly optimal plan because it maximizes the probability of detection for every k, and therefore minimizes the expected time to find the target if search is carried out until the target is found.

There is a probabilistic interpretation of the computations in Table 5-14. Let C_i be the event that the target is actually in cell i, and N_k be the event that there is no detection on any of the first k looks. In terms of these events, $p_i = P(C_i)$, and, if k_i is the number of looks out of k in cell i, $q_i^{k_i} = P(N_k | C_i)$. Therefore $P(N_k) = \sum_i P(N_k|C_i)\, P(C_i) = \sum_i p_i q_i^{k_i}$. In the example,

$$P(N_5) = .0625/(1-q_1) + .0512/(1-q_2) + 0/(1-q_3) = .125 + .256$$
$$= .381,$$

so the probability of detection after five looks is $1 - .381 = .619$. In general, the probability of detection after k looks can be determined from line k (the $k + 1^{st}$ line) in the table. Also,

$$P(C_i | N_k) = P(N_k | C_i)\, P(C_i)/P(N_k) = p_i q_i^{k_i} / P(N_k),$$

so the probabilities that the target is in each of the cells, given that the previous k looks have failed to find the target, are easily obtainable from row k. For example, the probability that the target is in cell 2 given 5 unsuccessful searches is $.256/.381 = .672$.

Sheet "Search" of *Search4.xls* is set up to perform these Bayesian calculations for an arbitrary discrete problem. The best cell to search is suggested, but the user is free to search any cell if he wishes. The numbers $1-q_i$ (which are called POD in land search) go in column 1, while the numbers p_i (called POA in land search) go in column 2. The displayed numbers will not match those of Table 5-14 because $P(C_i | N_k)$ is displayed in the spreadsheet, as is typical in search decision aids (see Chapter 7).

The above search policy follows the rule "always look in the cell where the probability of detecting the target on the next look is as large as possible". This sounds so sensible that its optimality is almost obvious. The rule will be called "myopic", since it is concerned exclusively with what happens on the next look, rather than with all future looks. The myopic rule is uniformly optimal for problems where the target is stationary. This is not so in cases where the target moves from cell to cell, as will be seen in Chapter 6.

5.5. Random Sweepwidth

In this section, a sensor's sweepwidth is assumed not to change during the search, but is nonetheless unknown in advance. This could happen if the condition of the target were unknown, for example, since sweepwidth depends as much on the target as on the sensor. The target could be more or less buried in the mud, or could possibly have built a smoky fire, or may have partially disintegrated on impact (this was an issue in the *Scorpion* search). We will assume that a sweepwidth probability density $g(W)$ is available, taking the Bayesian approach to the effort distribution problem.

If d is the effort density in the vicinity of the target, and if the sweepwidth is W, let $B(W,d)$ be the conditional probability of detection. Symbolically, if D is the event "detection", $P(D \mid W,d) = B(W,d)$. Then, if $f(x,y)$ is the probability density of the target's position,

$$P(D|W) = \iint f(x,y) P(D|W,d(x,y))dxdy ,\qquad (5.5\text{-}1)$$

where $d(x,y)$ is the effort density in the vicinity of (x,y), and

$$P(D) = \int P(D|W)g(W)dW = \iint f(x,y)b(d(x,y))dxdy ,\qquad (5.5\text{-}2)$$

where

$$b(d) = \int B(W,d)\,g(W)\,dW.\qquad(5.5\text{-}3)$$

The second equality in (5.5-2) is an interchange in the order of integration. Certain choices of the form of the density function $g(W)$ may simplify the calculation of the effective detection function $b(d)$. For example, if $B(W,d) = 1 - \exp(-VWd)$ as in random search, and if $g(W) = W^{\upsilon-1}\,\alpha^{\upsilon}\exp(-\alpha W)/\Gamma(\upsilon)$, which is a gamma density with convolution parameter $\upsilon > 0$ and scale parameter $\alpha > 0$, then

$$b(d) = 1 - (1 + Vd/\alpha)^{-\upsilon}.\qquad(5.5.4)$$

The problem of maximizing $P(D)$ when effort is constrained can be solved using a Lagrangian approach, as in Section 5.3. There are consequently no special techniques required to solve problems where sweepwidth is uncertain; conceptually, one simply averages the fixed sweepwidth detection function $B(W,d)$ to obtain a revised detection function $b(d)$, and then proceeds to work the allocation of effort problem without further reference to sweepwidth. Richardson and Belkin [2] have derived detailed results for the case of random search with gamma distributed sweepwidth in the cases where $f(x,y)$ is normal and uniform.

It is worthy of note that the revised detection function $b(d)$ is <u>not</u> $B(\overline{W},d)$, where $\overline{W}$ is the mean of the random sweepwidth. In fact, if $B(W,d)$ is a concave function of W, then $b(d) \le B(\overline{W},d)$ by Jensen's Inequality. It consequently takes longer to find the target in the random sweepwidth case than it does in the case where sweepwidth is fixed at $\overline{W}$; that is, it is optimistic to assume a fixed sweepwidth $\overline{W}$ when the sweepwidth is actually random. Richardson and Belkin [2] show that the ratio of the two mean times to detection is $(\upsilon + 1/3)/(\upsilon - 1)$ for random search of a normal prior when sweepwidth is gamma distributed and $\upsilon > 1$. This ratio is 5 when $\upsilon = 4/3$. When $\upsilon \leq 1$, the mean time to detection with a random sweepwidth is actually infinite.

CHAPTER 5. Exercises.

1. Fill in the next line of Table 5-14.

   ANSWER: .03125, .0512, 0, 2.

2. Construct a table similar to 5-5 for the case $n = 10$, $t = 10$, $p_i = .1$, and $\tau_i = 1 + i$. You will have to make an initial guess for λ. Whatever the guess, the final detection probability should be .22 and search should be carried out in the first six cells. You may wish to use sheet "Effort" of *Search4.xls* to accomplish this.

3. Construct a table similar to 5-14 for the case $n = 4$, $(p_1, p_2, p_3, p_4) = (.1, .2, .3, .4)$, and $q_1 = .6$ for all i. What are the first five cells to be searched in the uniformly optimal plan, and what is the detection probability after five looks?

   ANSWER: The detection probability after five looks should be .528. This result can also be obtained using sheet "Search" of Search4.xls.

4. Table 5-5 shows the optimal distribution of five time units of effort in a particular problem. Suppose that those five units of effort are divided into $5/\Delta$ "looks" of Δ units each, and the Greedy algorithm then applied with $q_i = \exp(-\Delta/\tau_i)$. What is the optimal sequence of looks and the resulting detection probability when $\Delta = 1$? Same question when $\Delta = .5$? Both answers should be smaller than in the continuous case. This problem can be solved by using sheet "Search" of *Search4.xls*, the main effort being to get the right formula in column 1.

   ANSWER: .178 for $\Delta = 1$ and .182 for $\Delta = .5$. The benefit for having $\Delta < .5$ is evidently in the fourth decimal place.

5. Suppose $V = 10$ knots, $t = 8$ hours, $\sigma_X = 10$ n. miles, $\sigma_Y = 20$ n. miles, and that the sensor is of the cookie-cutter type with $W = 5$ n. miles. What is the probability of detection for exhaustive, SOLR, and SULR searches?

   ANSWER: From 5.3-4, $z = (10)\,(5)\,(8)/(2\pi(10)\,(20)) = 1/\pi = .318$. The answers in the three cases are .273, .190, and .186, as can be verified from Figure 5-10.

6. Same as 5, except t is not given and the mean time to detection is desired.

   ANSWER: From the last paragraph of 5.3, $\tau = 8\pi$ hours, so the answers are 8π, 24π, and 28π hours in the three cases.

7. Same as 5, except inverse cube law sensor.

   ANSWER: It is not possible to search exhaustively with an inverse cube law sensor. Assuming that a spiral search with track spacing $S = W$ were made, probability of detection could be approximated by $(1 - \exp(-z))\,(2\Phi(\sqrt{\pi/2}) - 1) = .215$, with the second factor being "probability of detection given that the target is within the area searched" (Formula 2.4-6). The answers for either of the random searches would be close to the answer in Problem 6.

8. An airplane drops a canister of 1000 "stickers" in the hope that at least one sticker will hit a target with a 100 m^2 surface area. The canister opens and disperses the stickers in a strategically optimal but locally random fashion. The position of the target is known exactly, but the airplane makes an error with standard deviations (300 m, 100 m) in the

downrange and cross-range directions in dropping the canister. What is the probability that at least one sticker hits the target?

ANSWER: Since it is only relative distances that matter, the fact that the error is in dropping the canister rather than locating the target is immaterial. The fact that "hitting" rather than "detecting" is involved is also immaterial. So $z = (1000)$ $(100m^2)/(2\pi(100m)\,(300m)) = .53$, and (using 5.3-5), $p = .275$. If you wish to simulate this using the "SULR_SOLR" sheet of *Search4.xls*, let the look radius r be $1/\sqrt{\pi}$, so that $\pi r^2 = 1$, and let the vertical and horizontal standard deviations be 30 and 10. Dividing all length measurements by 10 will keep the diagram on the page.

REFERENCES

[1] Everett, H. 1963. Generalized Lagrange multiplier method for solving problems of optimum allocation of resources. *Oper. Res.* **11** 399–417.

[2] Richardson, H. R., B. Belkin. 1972. Optimal search with uncertain sweep width. *Oper. Res.* **20** 764–784.

[3] Richardson, H. R., L. D. Stone. 1971. Operations analysis during the underwater search for *Scorpion*. *Naval Res. Logist. Quart.* **18** 141–157.

[4] Stone, L. D. 1975. *Theory of Optimal Search*. INFORMS Linthicum, MD.

[5] Washburn, A. R. 1981. Note on constrained maximization of a sum. *Oper. Res.* **29** 2.

6. RANDOMLY MOVING TARGETS

Targets such as lost hikers and lifeboats may move considerable distances from the point of loss even as the search for them proceeds. The motion can be beneficial for the searcher in a confined area because it increases relative speed (Section 6.1) but it can also be harmful if it causes the searcher's effort to be spread over an ever increasing area (Section 6.2).

The target's motion is assumed independent of the search, not specifically directed toward escape. This means that the results of this chapter should not be applied to problems such as those considered in Sections 1.6, 2.3, and 2.5. The basic idea here is that the target is just wandering around. The material in Section 6.1 was developed in World War II [5], which separates it from the material in Section 6.2 by about 35 years.

6.1. Dynamic Enhancement

Consider the following situation: A searcher and a target each move independently and randomly at speeds V and U, respectively, in a region with area A. The quantity of interest is the random time T that it takes for the searcher to come within $W/2$ of the target for the first time. Based on experience with similar problems such as those in Chapter 2, it is natural to expect that T is exponential, and that $E(T) = A/VW$ when U is "small". More generally, we might expect that $E(T) = A/\tilde{V} W$, where $\tilde{V}$ is an "equivalent speed" that depends on U and V in such a manner that $\tilde{V} = V$ when $U = 0$. Since $\tilde{V} = V$ when $U = 0$, it should also be true that $\tilde{V} = U$ when $V = 0$. The reason for this is that the target can just as well be thought of as looking for the searcher in this problem as vice versa. Assuming that both participants make the same interpretation of "random motion", there would be no way for an observer to tell searcher from target. We expect $\tilde{V}$ to be a symmetric function of V and U.

The relative speed between searcher and target is $\sqrt{U^2 + V^2 - 2UV\cos\theta}$, where θ is the angle between the velocity vectors. Since θ is actually random, we might expect $\tilde{V}$ to be the average of this relative speed with respect to a uniform distribution on θ.

$$\tilde{V} = \frac{1}{2\pi} \int_0^{2\pi} \sqrt{U^2 + V^2 - 2UV\cos\theta} \, d\theta. \qquad (6.1\text{-}1)$$

After some trigonometric manipulations, one can show that

$$\tilde{V} = 2(V + U) \, E(K)/\pi, \qquad (6.1\text{-}2)$$

where $K = 2\sqrt{UV}/(U+V)$ and

$$E(K) = \int_0^{\pi/2} \sqrt{1 - K^2 \sin^2\phi} \, d\phi. \qquad (6.1\text{-}3)$$

The integral in 6.1-3 cannot be evaluated explicitly, being a complete elliptic integral of the second kind. $E(K)$ is a decreasing function of K, with $E(0) = \pi/2$ and $E(1) = 1$. K is always a number between zero and 1. When

$$U/V = .2, .5, \text{ or } 1.0$$

$$K = .745, .942, \text{ or } 1.000$$

$$E(K) = 1.32, 1.11, \text{ or } 1.00,$$

and $\quad \tilde{V}/V = 1.01, 1.06, \text{ or } 1.27.$

$\tilde{V}$ is always larger than the larger of U and V; in fact, $\tilde{V}$ is well approximated by the larger of U and V when U and V are considerably different.

The phenomenon summarized in equations 6.1-2 and 6.1-3 is known as dynamic enhancement, since the searcher's speed is effectively "enhanced" by the speed of the target. Note that the best speed for the target if he wishes to avoid detection is zero. A target that wishes to avoid detection might actually choose to move around at (say) $U = .2V$, on the grounds that this is enough motion to prevent an exhaustive search, but nonetheless increases the equivalent searcher speed by only 1%.

The searcher could achieve a relative speed $\sqrt{U^2 + V^2}$, which is greater than $\tilde{V}$, if his velocity were always perpendicular to that of the target. This is essentially what happens in patrolling a channel (Section 1.3). That strategy is not feasible here, since the searcher does not know the direction of the target's velocity.

6.2. Markov Motion — Myopic Search

The dynamic enhancement theory of Section 6.1 is not applicable to problems where the target's position at some benchmark in time is known with reasonable accuracy. In such problems, the main effect of target motion is a continual expansion of the region within which the target is likely to be located, with a consequent dilution of search effort as time goes by. To handle such problems, the approach of Section 5.4 can be generalized by adding the possibility that the target may move from cell to cell as the search proceeds. Specifically, let C be a set of "cells" within which the target is assumed to move according to the Markov transition rule

$$\Gamma(x,y,t) = \text{probability that a target in cell } x \text{ at} \qquad (6.2\text{-}1)$$
$$\text{time } t \text{ goes next to cell } y;$$
$$x \in C, y \in C, t = 1,2, \dots .$$

For example, C might be a two-dimensional discrete lattice and $\Gamma(x,y,t) = .25$ if and only if y is one of the four nearest neighbors of x, a two-dimensional random walk.

Let $P(x,t)$ be the probability that the target arrives at cell x at time t without being detected by any of the searches at times 1, 2, ..., $t-1$. $P(x,1)$ is assumed to be known for all x; this is the *a priori* distribution for the target's position, so $\sum_{x \in C} P(x,1) = 1$. If $q(x,t)$ is the probability that a target in cell x at time t will not be detected at time t, then $P(x,t)\, q(x,t)$ is the probability that the target arrives at cell x at time t without being detected by any of the searches at times 1, 2, ..., t. The quantities $q(x,t)$ are the decision variables in this problem. If $q(x,t)$ is selected to minimize $\sum_{x \in C} P(x,t)q(x,t)$ for each t, then the search is said to be *myopic*. This term is reasonable because selecting $q(x,t)$ in that manner is equivalent to maximizing the probability of detection on the tth search, given failure on the first $t-1$ searches, without any regard for the impact of the search at time t on the detection probability for searches at $t+1$, $t+2$, etc. This type of search is known to be optimal in search for a stationary target (Section 5.4).

Whether $q(x,t)$ is myopic or not, the target distribution at time $t+1$ is given by

$$P(y,t+1) = \sum_{x \in C} P(x,t)q(x,t)\,\Gamma(x,y,t); \quad y \in C, t \geq 1. \qquad (6.2\text{-}2)$$

Formula 6.2-2 is true because, if a target is to be at y at $t+1$ and undetected, then it must be undetected at some point x at time t, be undetected by the search at time t, and then move from x to y. Since $P(x,1)$ is known for all x, 6.2-2 can be used to determine $P(x,2)$ for all x, then $P(x,3)$ for all x, etc.

The definition of "cell" need not confine itself to spatial coordinates. A given cell might correspond to a specified location and velocity, for example, with the transition rule Γ including the possibility of acceleration. A probability distribution over cells could then be regarded as a joint distribution whose spatial marginal distribution could be displayed as a probability map. This expandability permits the development of realistic Markov motion models, but of course there is a cost—the size of C increases geometrically as new features are added to the cell definition. Fortunately Formula 6.2-2 is simple enough that modern computers are able to handle models with hundreds of thousands of states (see discussion of NODESTAR in Chapter 7).

A "cell" could even be a target track, complete with all relevant details over a time period that encompasses any contemplated search, and C could consist of all conceivable target tracks. The advantage of this point of view is that 6.2-2 amounts to $P(x,t + 1) = P(x,t)\, q(x,t);\ x \in C,\ t \ge 1;$ the function Γ simply reflects the idea that the target does not "move" (from one cell to another), and really does not need to be represented. The Coast Guard's CASP system is of this type (see Chapter 7). The potential disadvantage is that the size of C might need to be awkwardly large.

Since $s_m = \displaystyle\sum_{x \in C} P(x,m)q(x,m)$ is the probability of not detecting the target at any time before m, a natural goal is to minimize s_m for some fixed

m that corresponds to the amount of search time available. Myopic search does not achieve the minimum, as the following example illustrates:

Let $C = \{1,2,3\}$, and let the rule for motion be that in one step the target goes to cell 2 if it is in cell 1, or to cell 3 if it is in cell 2, or remains in cell 3 if it is already in cell 3. The searcher may examine either cell 1 or cell 2 at each turn, and is assumed to detect the target if and only if the target is in the searched cell. Assume $P(1,1) = .51$, $P(2,1) = .49$, and $P(3,1) = 0$. The myopic strategy searches cell 1 first, since $.51 > .49$. In this case a target initially in cell 2 will "escape" to cell 3, after which detection is impossible. So the myopic strategy achieves a .51 detection probability after 1 look or after any larger number of looks. However, the strategy of always looking in cell 2 has a detection probability of 1.0 after 2 looks. The myopic strategy misses optimality by almost a factor of 2 in this contrived example.

The reader may feel that examples such as the above would be impossible if there were no "safe" cell for the target. A safe cell is not actually required; it merely makes the generation of counterexamples easy. However, it can be said that the myopic strategy is typically not as bad as the above example portrays.

6.3. Markov Motion — Optimal Search

In addition to the functions defined in Section 6.2, let $Q(x,t)$ be the probability that a target at x at t will not be detected by any of the searches at $t + 1$, $t + 2$, ..., m, given no detection at 1, ..., t, with $Q(x,m) = 1$ for all x. Then

$$s_m = \sum_{x \in C} P(x,t) q(x,t) Q(x,t) \quad \text{for all } t. \tag{6.3-1}$$

Formula 6.3-1 is true because a target that is never detected must pass through some point x at t, must not be detected at t, and must also not be detected before or after t, so that the three factors in 6.3-1 correspond to not being detected in the "past", "present", or "future". The right-hand side of 6.3-1 appears to be a function of t, but is actually a constant (the probability of never detecting the target).

Since the motion is Markov, and since the position of the target is given in computing $Q(x,t)$, the condition that there be no detection at 1, ..., t in the definition of $Q(x,t)$ is actually immaterial. Therefore, for all x and $t \geq 2$,

$$Q(x,t-1) = \sum_{y \in C} \Gamma(x,y,t-1)q(y,t)Q(y,t). \qquad (6.3\text{-}2)$$

Equation 6.3-2 is true because if a target at x at $t-1$ is not to be detected at t, ..., m, then it must move to some point y at t, not be detected at y at t, and then not be detected at $t+1$, ..., m from y. Note that the simplest way to compute $Q(x,t)$ is by a "backwards" method; i.e., $Q(x,m) = 1$ is known for all x, so 6.3-2 can be used to determine $Q(x,m-1)$ for all x, etc., until finally $Q(x,1)$ is evaluated. This is opposite to the "forwards" method of computing $P(x,t)$ by 6.2-2, where one begins with $P(x,1)$ and ends with $P(x,m)$.

The search function $q(x,t)$ determines both $P(x,t)$ and $Q(x,t)$. $P(x,t)$ depends on $q(y,u)$ for all y and $u < t$, and $Q(x,t)$ depends on $q(y,u)$ for all y and $u > t$. Note that neither $P(x,t)$ nor $Q(x,t)$ depends on $q(y,t)$ for any y. Therefore the definition of $q(y,t)$ can be changed at an arbitrary time t without affecting $P(x,t)$ or $Q(x,t)$. In particular, let f be the feasible search function that minimizes $\sum\limits_{x \in C} P(x,t)f(x)Q(x,t)$ within whatever constraints

are imposed. Then the search function q' is at least as good as q, where

$$q'(y,u) = \begin{cases} q(y,u) & \text{if } u \neq t \\ f(y) & \text{if } u = t. \end{cases} \tag{6.3-3}$$

Thus, the ability to solve stationary search problems (which is what determination of f amounts to) leads directly to the ability to effect gradual improvements in dynamic problems. Given any search function q, one simply looks for a time t at which q is inferior to f, and then obtains the improved search function q' by substituting f for q at that time. The process can be repeated, except that it is necessary to use 6.2-2 and 6.3-2 to recompute $P'(x,t)$ and $Q'(x,t)$ corresponding to q' after each step. As a practical matter, it is efficient to consider the stationary optimization problems at times $t = 1, ..., m$, in that order. In that case the forward function P can be calculated from 6.2-2, while q' is determined from 6.3-3. Then 6.3-2 can be used to make all backward calculations of Q', thus completing one iteration of the FAB (Forward and Backward) algorithm [1, 13]. The initial Q-function can be set to 1.0 for all (x,t), which corresponds to the strategy of not searching at all; the initial P-function will then correspond to myopic search.

A strategy that cannot be improved by the above technique is called "critical". Criticality is a necessary condition for optimality. In some circumstances [1], it may also be sufficient. The following examples illustrate some of the possibilities.

Example 1.

Let C be the first 67 integers. The target moves in a discrete diffusion; from interior points it goes left or does not move or goes right with probabilities .3, .4, .3, respectively. From either of the two end positions, the target stays where it is or goes to the closest interior point with probabilities .4, .6, respectively. The target starts in cell 34 (the center) at time −2, so that it has moved three times by time 1, the first time when a cell is searched. Then, at each of 80 opportunities, the searcher searches at any one of the 67 integers; if the target is currently at that integer, the probability that it will not be detected is .85, or otherwise 1.0.

If the searcher were to pick an integer at random at each opportunity, the probability of non-detection would be $(1 - .15/67)^{80} = .8359$. The myopic strategy for this example has a nondetection probability of .3923. By successively improving it according to 6.3-3, a critical strategy with nondetection probability .3859 can be found. The myopic strategy is a large improvement on simply searching at random, while the critical strategy is a small improvement on the myopic strategy. The optimal strategy is unknown, but its nondetection probability cannot be smaller than .3731, as will be explained in the next example, so the myopic strategy is almost optimal.

Example 2.

The same as Example 1 except that the searcher is not restricted to looking in a single "cell" at each time. Specifically, he has 100 units of effort, and the probability of nondetection if z units of effort are spent in a cell is $\exp(-.001625z)$. If all 100 units are spent in a single cell, the nondetection probability is $\exp(-.1625) = .85$ as in Example 1, but the effort may be distributed over the cells in any manner whatever. In this case, it is known [1,3] that critical strategies are optimal because the objective function and the set of feasible strategies are both convex.

Iteration of the FAB algorithm 50 times produces a nondetection probability of .373078, known to be optimal to within 2×10^{-7} on account of the bound described in [12]. Since Example 2 is a relaxation of the problem considered in Example 1, .373078 is a lower bound on the nondetection probability that can be achieved in Example 1.

Figure 6-10 contrasts the myopic and optimal searches at time 50. It can be seen that the optimal distribution of effort (DOE) is more spread out; intuitively, the optimal strategy places some value on keeping the P-function concentrated in the center so that future searches will be efficient. Mechanically, the effort is more spread out because the Q-function has a minimum in the center where the P-function has a maximum.

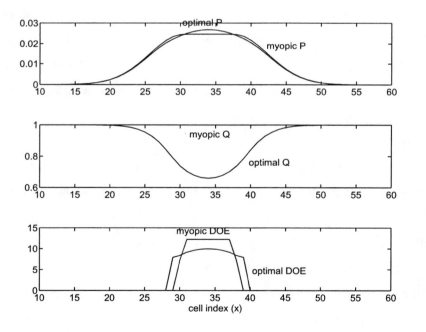

COMPARISON OF MYOPIC AND OPTIMAL SEARCHES AT TIME 50

Example 3.

The same as Example 1 except that the sequence of searched cells $x_1, ..., x_m$ is further restricted to have the property that $|x_i - x_{i+1}| \leq 1$ for $1 \leq i < m$, with $m = 80$. The idea is that a searcher in cell x can only search x or one of its neighbors on the next opportunity. The feasible search function $f(\ )$ used in 6.3-3 now amounts to a choice of cell that is consistent with both x_{t-1} and x_{t+1}. This can be quite restrictive; if $x_3 = 2$ and $x_5 = 4$, then the only feasible choice at time 4 is cell 3, for example. This "continuity" requirement causes the nondetection probability to increase relative to what it would be if x_t did not have to be consistent with earlier and later searches. The myopic computation requires x_t to be consistent only with x_{t-1}, but even so the myopic nondetection probability increases to .3971 from its level of .3923 in Example 1. The next FAB iteration reduces the nondetection probability to .3953, after which there are no further improvements. It is not known whether .3953 is optimal.

Example 3 is an "optimal searcher path" problem, to be distinguished from Examples 1 and 2 which are "optimal DOE" problems. DOE problems are easier to solve, but the solutions may have characteristics that a real searcher cannot implement. This DOE defect can occur even when the target is stationary, witness the lack of continuity in the sequence of cells searched in Table 5-14. The DOE formulation might be defended on the grounds that a real searcher will only be looking for a rough guide to action, rather than a well-defined path, but still there are circumstances where optimal search paths could be implemented if only they could be computed. Unfortunately, optimal searcher path problems appear to be fundamentally difficult [11]. In discrete problems, one approach to computing optimal paths is a Branch-and-Bound technique based on a DOE relaxation [2, 8, 14], but solvable problems at this writing are considerably smaller than Example 3.

In problems where the searcher's path is continuous, there have been some applications of optimal control theory [3, 6, 7] as well as some solutions of "conditionally deterministic" problems where the target's motion is deterministic except for a small number of parameters [9]. Heuristic methods such as genetic algorithms have also shown promise [4].

The Markov assumption can be dispensed with at some computational expense. Stone [10] gives necessary and sufficient conditions for optimality.

CHAPTER 6. Exercises

1. What mean time to detection would the dynamic enhancement theory of Section 6.1 predict for the experiment discussed in Section 2.5 and portrayed in Figure 2-14? Explain the large difference between this prediction and the measured mean time of 367 seconds.

   ANSWER: 267 seconds is too small because the evader's motion is not independent of the pursuer's, and consequently the angle θ in 6.1-1 is not uniformly distributed.

2. Identify $\Gamma(x,y,t)$ for the three cell example discussed in Section 6.2.

   ANSWER: $\Gamma(1,2,t) = \Gamma(2,3,t) = \Gamma(3,3,t) = 1$ for $t = 1,2, ...$; otherwise, $\Gamma(x,y,t) = 0$.

3. Let $C = \{1,2,3,4,5\}$, $P(2,1) = P(3,1) = P(4,1) = 1/3$, $\Gamma(5,5,t) = \Gamma(1,1,t) = \Gamma(5,4,t) = \Gamma(1,2,t) = 1/2$. For $x = 2,3,4$, $\Gamma(x,x,t) = 1/2$, $\Gamma(x,x + 1,t) = \Gamma(x,x - 1,t) = 1/4$. For all x, $q(x,t) = 1/2$ if cell x is searched at time t, or $q(x,t) = 1$ otherwise.

   a) Start a myopic search in cell 3. What is $P(x,2)$ for $x = 1, ..., 5$?

   b) Start a myopic search in cell 4. What is $P(x,2)$ for $x = 1, ..., 5$?

   c) Is case a) or b) better for maximizing the detection probability after 2 looks?

   ANSWER: $P(x,2) = (2/24, 5/24, 6/24, 5/24, 2/24)$ for $x = 1,2,3,4,5$ in a), and

   $P(x,2) = (2/24, 6/24, 7/24, 4/24, 1/24)$ in b).

   Case b) is better, since the detection probability after 2 looks $(1 - s_2)$ is 15/48 in that case, vice 14/48 if cell 3 is searched first.

4. What is $Q(x,t)$ for the myopic search in Exercise 3a) if $m = 2$? (Since $Q(x,m) = 1$, the only computations to be made are for $t = 1$.) Is the myopic search of 3a) critical? Is the myopic search of 3b) critical?

ANSWER: $Q(x,1) = (8/8, 7/8, 6/8, 7/8, 8/8)$ for $x = 1,2,3,4,5$ in 3a), and hence

$Q(x,1) \, P(x,1) = (0, 7/24, 6/24, 7/24, 0)$.

Since $6/24$ is not maximal, the myopic strategy of 3a) is not critical (and therefore not optimal). The same computations hold in 3b), and the myopic strategy of 3b is therefore critical. As a matter of fact, it is also optimal.

5. A target can be in one of five locations, and can have one of two velocities. The transition function $\Gamma(x,y,t)$ is shown in the diagram below, using the code that an arrow from cell x to cell y means that $\Gamma(x,y,t)$ is the number written beside the arrow for all t (all transitions with no arrow are impossible). F1 is a fast target at location 1, S3 is a slow target at location 3, etc. All 10 cells are equally likely at time 1, and at time 1 a search is made that will detect a target in cell F2, F3 or F4 with probability .5, or with probability 0 in any other cell.

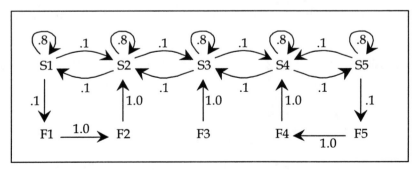

a) What is $P(x,2)$? Give the answer as a 10-vector beginning with S1 and ending with F5.

ANSWER: (.09, .15, .15, .15, .09, .01, .1, 0, .1, .01)

b) $\sum_{x \in C} P(x,2)$ is not 1. What is the meaning of that sum?

c) What is the probability that the target is in location 1 at time 2 <u>and</u> is not detected at time 1? Same question for locations 2, 3, 4, 5.

ANSWER: (.1, .25, .15, .25, .1)

d) Most tactical decision aids would replace the word "and" by "given" in the previous question before displaying a probability distribution over location. What needs to be done to the answer to c) to obtain this distribution?

REFERENCES

[1] Brown, S. S. 1980. Optimal search for a moving target in discrete time and space. *Oper. Res.* **28** 1275–1289.

[2] Eagle, J. N., J. R. Yee. 1990. An optimal branch-and-bound procedure for the constrained path, moving target search problem. *Oper. Res.* **38** 110–114.

[3] Hellman, O. 1970. On the effect of a search upon the probability distribution of a target whose motion is a diffusion process. *Ann. Math. Statist.* **41** 1717–1724.

[4] Kierstead, D., D. DelBalzo. 2001. A genetic algorithm approach for planning search paths in complicated environments. *Military Oper. Res.* Forthcoming.

[5] Koopman, B. O. 1980. *Search and Screening.* Pergamon Press, New York.

[6] Lukka, M. 1977. On the optimal searching track for a moving target. *SIAM J. Appl. Math.* **32** 126–132.

[7]   Ohsumi, A. 1986. Optimal searching for a markovian target and relation to optimal stochastic control. C. I. Byrnes and A. Lindquist, eds. *Theory and Applications of Nonlinear Control Systems.* Elsevier, Amsterdam, The Netherlands. 569–582.

[8]   Stewart, T. J. (1979), "Search for a Moving Target When Searcher Motion is Restricted", *Comput. Oper. Res.* **6**, 129–140.

[9]   Stone, L. D. 1977. Search for targets with generalized conditionally deterministic motion. *SIAM J. Appl. Math.* **33** 456–468.

[10] Stone, L. D. 1979. Necessary and sufficient conditions for optimal search plans for moving targets. *Math. Oper. Res.* **4** 431–440.

[11] Trummel, K. E., J. R. Weisinger. 1986. The complexity of the optional searcher path problem. *Oper. Res.* **34** 324–327.

[12] Washburn, A. R. 1981. An upper bound useful in optimizing search for a moving target. *Oper. Res.* **29** 1226–1230.

[13] Washburn, A. R. 1983. Search for a moving target: The FAB algorithm. *Oper. Res.* **31** 739–751.

[14] Washburn, A. R. 1998. Branch and Bound Methods for a Search Problem. Naval res. Logist. **45** 243–257.

7. APPLICATIONS AND SOFTWARE

The concepts presented in preceding chapters are useful as a mental framework, even when not applied formally, but formal applications are still the most direct evidence for usefulness. The object of this chapter is to review some of these applications, paying particular attention to tactical decision aids. The situation on land is different from the situation at sea, so a subsection is devoted to each topic.

7.1.   Tactical Decision Aids (TDAs)

A human has two problems in conducting an extended search, be it for car keys or life raft. The first is to construct a coherent picture of the search's "status", taking into account all of the states in which the target might be and the implications of past search activity. This can be difficult, especially if the target is moving. The second problem is to decide what kind of searching to do next, a decision that should be based on the status assessment. One can imagine a search proceeding in a succession of phases, with each phase involving an assessment (the first problem) and a decision (the second).

Search TDAs are usually organized around the idea of helping with the assessment problem primarily by drawing a succession of probability maps, one for each phase. Such maps can be portrayed in many ways. One way is shown in Figure 5-2. That map might also have been shown digitally (as it was originally), as a contour map, in color, or in any other way suitable for displaying a topographic map or chart. By continually revising such maps to show the effects of past search activities, the TDA gives its user a good idea of the search's "status", while simultaneously prompting him to conduct further search wherever the probabilities are largest. Assigning this task to the computer has proved to be an effective way of using its extensive computational and graphical abilities to solve the assessment problem.

Computers are also potentially of use in solving the decision optimization problem, but so far optimization has played a relatively minor role. There are several reasons. The probability map motivates a myopic approach where the maximum amount of probability is "covered" in each phase, a two-dimensional pattern recognition problem that humans are good at. It is true that myopia is not optimal when the target is moving, but even then it usually doesn't miss by much (recall Examples 1 and 2 at the end of Chapter 6). Another reason is that the abstract problem of allocating search effort optimally can be difficult, even for a computer, by the time realistic constraints on action are incorporated (recall Example 3 at the end of Chapter 6).

Except for minor deviations, all moving target TDAs operate as described in Section 6.2. The user specifies a prior distribution and motion model for the target, the function $q(x,t)$ is determined by a built-in physical model and the user's search decisions, and Formula 6.2-2 is used iteratively to update the probability map. However, the details will be easier to explain with some additional notation. Specifically, let

$$P^+(x,t) = P(x,t)q(x,t) \Big/ \sum_{y \in C} P(y,t)q(y,t); \qquad x \in C; t \geq 1. \qquad (7.1\text{-}1)$$

$P^+(x,t)$ is the probability that the target is in cell x, given that all previous searches fail to find the target, including the search at time t. Formula 6.2-2 is replaced by 7.1-1 and its companion

$$P(y,t+1) = \sum_{x \in C} P^+(x,t)\Gamma(x,y,t); \qquad y \in C; t \geq 1. \qquad (7.1\text{-}2)$$

7-2

$P(y,t + 1)$ is the probability that the target is in cell y at time $t + 1$, given no detection at time t or before, the quantity portrayed in the aforementioned probability maps. Formula 7.1-1 will be called the detection model, since the function $q(x,t)$ is determined by the user's decisions (optimal or not) about how to search. Formula 7.1-2 will be called the motion model, since the function $\Gamma(x,y,t)$ describes how the target moves. Replacement of 6.2-2 with 7.1-1 and 7.1-2 makes it plain that a TDA must have two distinct submodels, one for search and one for target motion. The division in 7.1-1 could be avoided, since it is simply a scale factor forcing the product $P(x,t)$ $q(x,t)$ to sum (on x) to 1.0, but it is retained in TDAs because $P(x,t)$ and $P^+(x,t)$ are more easily interpreted as conditional distributions that sum to 1 than as joint distributions that sum to less than 1, as $P(x,t)$ did in Chapter 6.

If the description of the target state is sufficiently detailed, a motion model may not be necessary. This obviously applies if the target does not move, but it also applies to moving targets if the state is a "track" that specifies location and other properties (velocity, detectability, live/dead, etc.) as a function of time. In either case, 7.1-2 is not needed and $P^+(x,t)$ in 7.1-1 can be replaced by $P(x,t + 1)$.

The user of a search TDA must provide information about the initial location of the target and, if appropriate, information about how the target moves, but usually not on a cell-by-cell basis. Alternatives for the initial distribution might be to specify the corners of a polygon within which the target's position is uniformly distributed, or the parameters of an elliptical normal distribution. The function $P(x,1)$ is then calculated based on the user's input. Similarly, the user will make statements about the nature of the target, including perhaps its speed and tendency to turn, after which

$\Gamma(x,y,t)$ is calculated by the TDA. The principle is to speak the user's language whenever possible, translating his statements into mathematical form as required. The user may also have to provide some inputs for the search model. After making these initial inputs, however, the user can concentrate entirely on tactics. The task of translating tactics into the function $q(x,t)$ required in 7.1-1, as well as all of the subsequent arithmetic, is left to the TDA.

The function $q(x,t)$ has been described as the probability of the event E = "target not detected", given that it is in cell x at time t. However, the same Bayesian manipulations are appropriate regardless of the definition of E, as long as E is conditionally independent of past observations and there is a scientific basis for calculating $q(x,t)$. Some TDAs take advantage of this situation by permitting E to represent various kinds of "positive" information, as well as the "negative" information implied by nondetection. The target might be detected, for example, but not accurately enough to terminate the search, or perhaps a clue of some sort might be found. This leads to alternative calculations of $q(x,t)$, but 7.1-1 (Bayes Theorem) is still fundamental.

7.2   Maritime Search

Search Theory was developed in World War II with primarily nautical applications in mind, and most of the applications since then have continued to be nautical. The open literature includes two of these—the 1968 search for the lost submarine *Scorpion* [6], and the more recent search for the *Central America* [7], a ship that sank in 1857 with hundreds of millions of dollars worth of gold. Both of these successful applications emphasize the careful development of a prior distribution for target location, quantitative sensor descriptions through lateral range curves, and selection of a search plan to maximize detection probability. The same techniques were also used in searching for a lost H-bomb in 1964. Each of these is a search for a stationary target sufficiently important to justify the development of prior distributions and sensor descriptions in unique circumstances. Less well known, but more important in their entirety, are applications to the search for moving targets by the Coast Guard and the Navy.

The Coast Guard handles thousands of search and rescue (SAR) incidents every year. Those that require search are infrequent, but nonetheless consume significant quantities of resources (people, search platforms, funds). It is therefore important to the Coast Guard to be efficient in searching for vessels or individuals lost at sea. Fortunately, the environmental knowledge required for a scientific approach to the problem is available. The Navy makes wind forecasts available, and the influence of the resulting forces on drifting objects is well understood. The capabilities of eyeball and radar in detecting objects on the surface of the ocean have been the object of experimentation since World War II. The Coast Guard has taken advantage of this knowledge by encoding it within a computer program called CASP [3,5]. CASP became operational in 1974, and a modified version is still in use at this writing. CASP begins its analysis by performing about 10,000 replications of a Monte Carlo simulation, each of which produces a plausible target track (so the set C in 7.1-1 is actually a set of about 10,000 tracks). Subsequent search modifies the track probabilities according to 7.1-1, with 7.1-2 not being needed because the target is "stationary" in the sense that it follows only a single track. By 1980, CASP had been credited with saving over a dozen lives [5].

Like the Coast Guard, the Navy has an abiding interest in maritime search for moving targets, and has developed computerized tactical decision aids (TDAs) for the function. The Navy's target is usually an uncooperative submarine; in a typical problem the existence and rough location of a submarine are first revealed by long-range sonar arrays, after which aircraft attempt to establish contact with other sensors.

Many of the Navy's search TDAs have been developed by Daniel H. Wagner, Assoc., the founder and namesake of which company has included a history of TDA development in [10]. The first Naval TDAs appeared at about the same time as CASP, and used similar methods. Naval TDAs differ from CASP primarily in that detections are by sonar, with all of the implied dependence on the sound structure of the ocean. Invariably they capitalize on the pre-existence of methods for forecasting sonar signal excess, which is converted to a single-look detection probability, which in turn becomes the basis of a CDP calculation as in Section 3.1. The nondetection probability $1 - CDP$ is then used in making the Bayesian update. Some Naval TDAs have retained CASP's use of tracks, while others have employed Markov chain methods. One example of the Markov chain approach is NODESTAR [8]. This TDA uses a six-dimensional cell description: three components (including depth) for position, two components (without depth) for velocity, and one for target class (detectability and motion both depend on whether a target submarine has a nuclear power plant, for example). The definition of "cell" is actually dynamic and depends on circumstances, but there may be 500,000 in total. NODESTAR can track multiple targets simultaneously, and even has some data-association capability. At bottom, however, it employs 7.1-1 and 7.1-2 to do Bayesian updating.

There was a period of time in the late 1970s when the Navy planned antisubmarine flights from Moffett Field both with and without OASIS, the TDA that was available at the time. This was a rare opportunity for testing whether the use of computers actually resulted in detecting more submarines. Benkoski [1] collected data from January 1977 to April 1978 and reported the fraction of successful flights for each method. Several definitions of "success" were tested, but regardless of the definitions the OASIS success probability (about 70%) was about double the fraction achieved using conventional flight planning methods (about 35%). This remarkable increase in effectiveness confirms the difficulty of planning search operations "by hand", particularly when the target is moving, as well as the utility of TDAs such as OASIS.

7.3 Inland Search

The regular application of Search Theory seems to require the regular occurrence of a search problem that is important enough to have an organization devoted to it. At sea, SAR incidents are handled by the Coast Guard, and hostile submarines are searched for by the Navy. Maritime TDAs are used for other purposes (CASP has even been used on land), but they would never even have been developed without those two classes of problem.

Search problems also occur regularly on land, notably the search for crashed aircraft (stationary targets) and for individuals who have simply become lost (moving targets). However, the inland SAR situation is essentially different from the maritime situation in that many more organizations are involved. The Coast Guard actually <u>does</u> most of the maritime SAR, whereas inland SAR is conducted by a host of organizations, many of them voluntary, that includes the Civil Air Patrol, the county sheriff's office, the National Park Service, the Boy Scouts, and many others. The Federal Aviation Administration does not provide search manpower, but is likely to be the source of information about missing aircraft. The Air Force Rescue Coordination Center coordinates all of this potential SAR information and manpower, paying due attention to individual agreements with each state, committing expensive Air Force assets only as a last resort.

Training for inland search is done mainly by the National Search and Rescue School in Yorktown, VA, which maintains a traveling short course. In addition, the National Association for Search and Rescue (NASAR) and the Emergency Response Institute (ERI) each have training functions and bookstores. The following formula for the Probability of Success (POS) is employed consistently in this training:

$$\text{POS} = \sum_{j=1}^{n} \text{POA}_j \ \ \text{POD}_j, \qquad (7.3\text{-}1)$$

where j indexes a partition of the search space into n cells, POA_j is the probability that the target is in fact in cell j ("Probability of Area"), and POD_j is the conditional Probability of Detection, given that the target is in cell j. This formula is included in [4], for example, which also discusses how to "shift" (update via Bayes Theorem) the POAs as search proceeds. Thus the fundamental Bayesian paradigm is the same in both maritime and inland search. However, the two differ in that the idea of a motion model seems to be missing in inland search; that is, POAs do not "shift" merely on account of the passage of time. This is in spite of the fact that studies [9] have been made of how lost individuals move around. Here are some speculative reasons for the omission:

1) The diffuse nature of the responsibility for inland search leaves it without a sponsor for development of either theory or software.

2) In the time available for training part time volunteers, Equation 7.3-1 is the most that can be reliably taught.

3) Inland search must cope with the effects of terrain, a complication that is missing in maritime search.

In any case, as of this writing, all inland search tutorial materials and TDAs are mute on the question of how to handle target motion quantitatively.

Possibly for the same three reasons, inland search TDAs such as CASIE3 [2] are in most respects more primitive than their maritime counterparts. In CASIE3 the initial POAs are input digitally on a cell-by-cell basis. PODs must also be input directly by the user. CASIE3 treats the target as stationary, even though narrative information about how various targets move is available on a pull-down menu. CASIE3 is a user-friendly TDA that has been well received in the inland SAR community, and which reliably shifts the POAs to account for past search effort. Nonetheless, it is primitive compared to CASP or NODESTAR.

CASIE3 does have one feature not present in maritime TDAs, a feature directly related to the fact that inland search is often conducted by heterogeneous assets (dogs, helicopters, ...) in varied terrain. POD is actually doubly subscripted, with POD_{jk} being the detection probability of asset k in cell j, and POS is given by

$$POS = \sum_{j=1}^{n} POA_j \left[1 - \prod_k (1 - POD_{jk})^{X_{jk}} \right], \qquad (7.3\text{-}2)$$

where X_{jk} is 1 or zero depending on whether asset k is assigned to cell j or not. This brings up the question of how to assign assets to cells in order to maximize POS. For small numbers of assets and cells, CASIE3 finds the solution by exhaustion. Washburn [11] describes a branch-and-bound method for solving somewhat larger problems.

Whatever the explanation for the current lack of sophistication in inland search theory and TDAs, and whatever the organizational difficulties of achieving a remedy, it is probably true that better TDAs in the hands of well trained inland search managers would find more targets. There is evidence of such improvements for both the Navy and the Coast Guard in the maritime case. Inland search, with a larger incident base and additional complicating features such as the effects of terrain, should be an even better candidate for improvement.

REFERENCES

[1] Benkoski, S. 1978. Optimal use of the operational ASW search information system. Commander Patrol Wings Atlantic Fleet Lessons Learned. 261–279.

[2] CASIE3. NASAR P.O. Box 3709, Fairfax, VA and ERI 4537 Foxhall Dr. NE, Olympia, WA.

[3] Haley, K., L. Stone, eds. 1980. *Search Theory and Applications.* Plenum, New York.

[4] LaValla, P., R. Stoffel, A. Jones. 1995. *Search Is an Emergency*, ERI 4537 Foxhall Dr. NE, Olympia, WA.

[5] Richardson, H., J. Dicenza. 1980. The United States Coast Guard Computer-Assisted Search Planning System (CASP). *Naval Res. Logist.* **27** 659–680.

[6] Richardson, H. R., L. D. Stone. 1971. Operations analysis during the underwater search for *Scorpion. Naval Res. Logist. Quart.* **18** 141–157.

[7] Stone, L. D. 1992. Search for the *SS Central America*: Mathematical treasure hunting. *Interfaces* **22** 32–54.

[8] Stone, L., T. Corwin. 1995. NODESTAR: A nonlinear, discrete, multiple-target, correlator-tracker: Part 1. *US Navy J. Underwater Acoustics* **45**.

[9] Syrotuck, W. 1977. *Analysis of Lost Person Behaviour.* NASAR P.O. Box 3709, Fairfax, VA.

[10] Wagner, D. 1989. Naval tactical decision aids. NPSOR-90-01, Naval Postgraduate School, Monterey, CA.

[11] Washburn, A. 1995. Branch and bound methods for search problems. NPSOR-95-003, Naval Postgraduate School, Monterey, CA.

8. LOCALIZATION AND TRACKING

Search is always carried out with the idea of taking some subsequent action, and the success of this action usually hinges on how accurately the target's position is known. In this chapter we take a detailed look at the question of accuracy, with emphasis on the case where position is to be determined from multiple bearings.

8.1. Confidence Regions

Unless they happen to be parallel, two lines of bearing (LOB's) will always intersect at a unique "fix". When there are three LOB's, however, measurement errors typically prevent the three lines from intersecting at one point, and a triangle or "cocked hat" results (solid lines in Figure 8-2). Even though the third line should in principle make position estimation more accurate, its presence may actually lead to confusion, since it is no longer obvious where to place the "fix". Section 8.2 includes a discussion of exactly where the fix should be placed; for the moment, consider only the simpler question of how likely it is that the random cocked hat actually contains the stationary target.

In Figure 8-2, the case where the target is to the right of each of three LOB's *a, b,* and *c* is illustrated with solid lines (the RRR case). The dashed lines show the RLR case where the target is to the left (L) of line b but to the right (R) of lines a and c. In the RRR case, the target is in the cocked hat, but not in the RLR case. There are actually eight cases, in only two of which (RRR and LLL) is the target within the cocked hat; this will always be true as long as none of the three lines are parallel. Reversal of the direction of some of the lines would change the names of the two cases, but there would still be two. If each line is equally likely to pass to

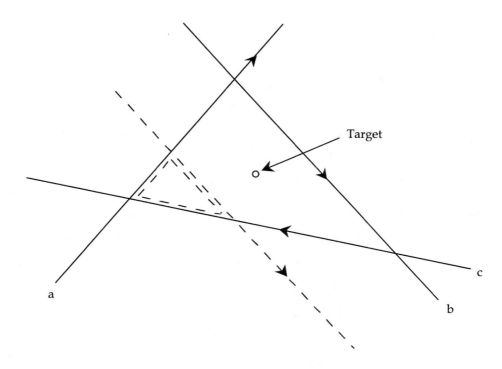

FORMATION OF A RANDOM COCKED HAT

WITH RESPECT TO A FIXED TARGET

the right or left of the target, then evidently only 2/8 of all cocked hats contain the target. With only three LOB's, the cocked hat is therefore not a very powerful confidence region. This result is intuitively surprising. In [1], Stansfield reports of his World War II experience that, "My own experience was with squadron leaders; they were ...surprised when they were told that there was a 3 to 1 chance that the actual position was outside the 'triangle of error'—they knew by the light of nature that the actual position was somewhere within it".

With more than three LOB's, the cocked hat generalized to be the largest possible closed polygon has a better chance of containing the target. Figure 8-3 shows the case of four LOB's. There are eight polygonal segments that extend to infinity and three that do not. The "cocked hat" is the union of the three that do not. Daniels [1] gives $1 - n/2^{n-1}$ as the formula for the fraction of cocked hats containing targets when there are n LOB's; this fraction is .5 when $n = 4$.

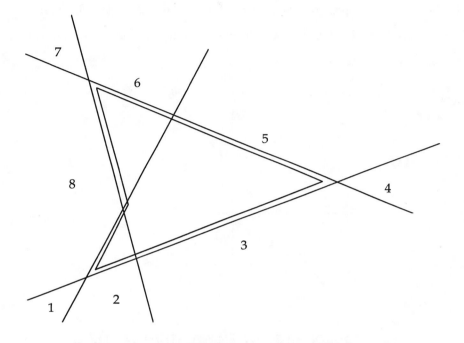

A COCKED HAT FORMED BY FOUR BEARING LINES

The above analyses compute the fraction of cocked hats that enclose the target, given only that lines of position are equally likely to be on either side of the target. If *a priori* error distributions on the lines of position are known, the probability that a <u>given</u> cocked hat contains the target could in principle be computed by integrating the joint error distribution over the cocked hat. The larger the cocked hat, of course, the more likely that it contains the target.

8.2.　Least Squares Point Estimates

In a fixed $x - y$ coordinate system, each line of bearing (LOB) can be characterized by two numbers θ and d, with θ being the angle counter-clockwise from the x-axis to the LOB and $|d|$ being the smallest distance to the origin. d is positive if the origin lies to the right as an observer moves past it in the direction θ, otherwise negative. Figure 8-4 illustrates the case where $(\theta,d) = (\pi/4, 1)$.

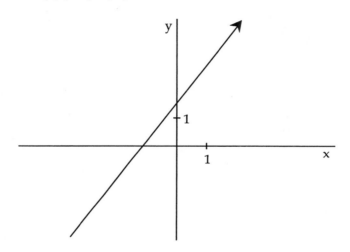

X-Y COORDINATE SYSTEM WITH THE (π/4, 1) LOB

The squared distance from an arbitrary point (x,y) to the (θ,d) line is $(x \sin \theta - y \cos \theta + d)^2$. If there are actually n lines of bearing with parameters θ_j and d_j, then the least squares estimate or "fix" is the point (x,y) that minimizes the penalty function $L(x,y)$:

$$L(x,y) = \sum_{j=1}^{n}\left(x \sin\theta_j - y\cos\theta_j + d_j\right)^2 \Big/ \sigma_j^2 . \qquad (8.2\text{-}1)$$

Except for the parameters σ_j, $L(x,y)$ is just the sum of all the squared miss distances. The parameters σ_j can be used to increase or decrease the effect of a particular line; if line 2 is known to be a particularly accurate measurement, for example, then σ_2 should be smaller than the others. By equating the two partial derivatives to zero, it can be shown that the minimizing point (x,y) is the solution of

$$ax + hy = f$$
$$hx + by = g$$

where

$$a = \sum_{j=1}^{n} \sin^2 \theta_j \big/ \sigma_j^2$$

$$b = \sum_{j=1}^{n} \cos^2 \theta_j \big/ \sigma_j^2 \qquad\qquad (8.2\text{-}2)$$

$$h = -\sum_{j=1}^{n} \sin \theta_j \cos \theta_j \big/ \sigma_j^2$$

$$f = -\sum_{j=1}^{n} d_j \sin \theta_j \big/ \sigma_j^2$$

$$g = \sum_{j=1}^{n} d_j \cos \theta_j \big/ \sigma_j^2 .$$

It is worthy of note that the five constants a, b, h, f, and g that are involved in the pair of simultaneous equations for (x,y) are all sums. The action required when adding a new line of bearing is therefore to "update" the five numbers by adding another term, rather than to start all over again.

The point (x,y) can be thought of as a best guess at the position of the target. In order to quantify how good the guess is, it is necessary to provide a probabilistic interpretation of 8.2-2. This is the subject of the next section.

8.3. Normal Error Ellipses

Let (X, Y) be the actual position of the target, assumed to have a two-dimensional density function that is *a priori* flat over a large area; i.e., we initially have no idea where the target is. Assume further that the line through (X, Y) in the direction θ_j is displaced from the jth LOB by a normal error with mean zero and variance σ_j^2, with all n of these errors being independent. Then the density function of (X, Y), given the information in the n lines of bearing, is normal with mean (x,y) and inverse covariance matrix

$$\Sigma^{-1} = \begin{pmatrix} a & h \\ h & b \end{pmatrix},$$

with x, y, a, b, and h being as in 8.2-2. The proof of this statement via Bayes Theorem will be omitted. Evidently, a, b, and h have something to do with the quality of the estimate (x,y). The relationship is clearer in a rotated coordinate system. Relative to a coordinate system with origin at (x,y) rotated through a special angle θ, (X, Y) has variances s_1^2 and s_2^2 in the rotated x and y directions, with the two components being independent, given the n LOB's. The formulas for θ, s_1^2 and s_2^2 are

$$s_1^2 = \left[\left(\frac{a+b}{2}\right) - \sqrt{\left(\frac{a-b}{2}\right)^2 + h^2}\,\right]^{-1}$$

$$s_2^2 = \left[\left(\frac{a+b}{2}\right) + \sqrt{\left(\frac{a-b}{2}\right)^2 + h^2}\,\right]^{-1}$$

$$\theta = \begin{cases} \dfrac{1}{2}\tan^{-1}\left(\dfrac{2h}{a-b}\right) & \text{if } a < b \\[2ex] \dfrac{1}{2}\tan^{-1}\left(\dfrac{2h}{a-b}\right) + \dfrac{\pi}{2} & \text{if } a > b \\[2ex] \dfrac{\pi}{4} & \text{if } a = b \text{ and } h < 0 \\[2ex] -\dfrac{\pi}{4} & \text{if } a = b \text{ and } h >:0 \\[2ex] \text{arbitrary} & \text{if } a = b \text{ and } h = 0. \end{cases}$$

(8.3-1)

Note that $s_1 \geq s_2$ in all cases, so that the rotated x direction is the major axis of the family of equiprobability ellipses.

For example, suppose $n = 3$, with $(\theta_1, d_1) = (\pi/4, 2.828)$; $(\theta_2, d_2) = (0,3)$; and $(\theta_3, d_3) = (\pi, -1)$, as shown in Figure 8-8. Suppose further that $\sigma_1 = \sigma_2 = \sigma_3 = 1$. Then, using 8.2-2,

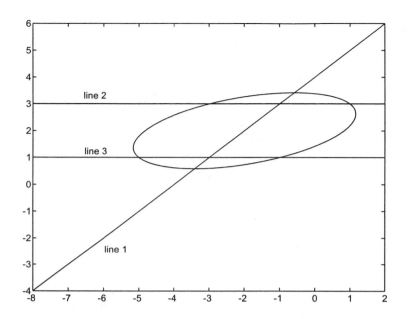

THREE BEARING LOCALIZATION

$$a = .5$$

$$b = 2.5$$

$$h = -.5$$

$$f = -(2.828)(.707) = -2.00$$

$$g = (2.828)(.707) + 3(1) + (-1)(-1) = 6.00$$

$$x = (fb - hg)/(ab - h^2) = -2.00$$

$$y = (ag - hf)/(ab - h^2) = 2.00$$

$$s_1 = 1.62$$

(8.3-2)

$$s_2 = .62$$

$$\theta = \frac{1}{2}\tan^{-1}(.5) = .232 \text{ radians } = 13.3 \text{ degrees.}$$

The center of the ellipse shown in Figure 8-8 is at $(x,y) = (-2, 2)$, and the major axis of the ellipse is inclined at $\theta = 13.3$ degrees. The ellipse shown is by convention a two-sigma ellipse; that is, the major half diameter is $2s_1$ and the minor half diameter is $2s_2$. By integrating the two-dimensional normal density function, it can be shown (see Formula 5.3-8) that a k-sigma ellipse contains the target with probability $p = 1-\exp(-k^2/2)$. When $k = 2$, $p = .865$, so the ellipse shown in Figure 8-8 contains the target with probability .865. No matter how big the ellipse, there is some chance that the target is outside; the ellipse is simply a convenient graphical way of communicating the five parameters (a, b, h, f, g) or (x, y, θ, s_1, s_2) that characterize a two-dimensional normal distribution.

The area inside a k-sigma ellipse is $A \equiv \pi k^2 s_1 s_2$. Solve this for k^2 and substitute into the expression for p. The result is

$$p = 1 - \exp\left(-\frac{A}{2\pi s_1 s_2}\right). \tag{8.3-3}$$

Formula 8.3-3 is the same as Formula 5.3-8. The product $s_1 s_2$ is just $(ab-h^2)^{-1/2}$, and can be computed directly using [1]

$$ab - h^2 = \sum_{i=1}^{n} \sum_{j=1}^{i} \sin^2(\theta_i - \theta_j) \Big/ (\sigma_i^2 \sigma_j^2). \tag{8.3-4}$$

The target will be well localized if $ab - h^2$ is large. Formula 8.3-4 makes it clear that achieving an accurate localization will be easiest if the bearings differ substantially among themselves. Of course it also helps if the standard deviations $\sigma_1, ..., \sigma_n$ are small.

The quantity σ_j has been described as the standard deviation of the amount by which the true LOB along θ_j is translated to get the measured LOB. In practice, θ_j is usually the random quantity, and the true LOB goes through the same observer as the measured one. Let w_j be the standard deviation of the angular error committed by the jth observer in radians, and r_j the approximate range from the jth observer to the target. Then the previous computations are accurate if $\sigma_j = w_j r_j$, provided w_j is not larger than a few degrees. If any of the numbers w_j are large, the density function of (X, Y) is not normal, and the previous calculations do not apply.

The origin of coordinates is arbitrary in all of the previous computations, but for numerical reasons it is best to place the origin at a rough guess of the target's position; otherwise, one will end up subtracting two large numbers that are nearly equal in computing (x,y).

In summary, the information in n LOB's can be summarized by five numbers. The a, b, h, f, g scheme is simplest for computations, since each number is a simple sum. The five numbers are more easily interpreted if they are converted to the x, y, θ, s_1, s_2 scheme, from which uncertainty ellipses can be sketched.

The reader is referred to [1] for a more complete discussion.

The calculations described in this section are implemented in sheet "DirFind" of the workbook *Search4.xls*.

8.4. Range Measurements

Suppose that the jth measurement is a range measurement accurate to within a normal error with standard deviation σ_j. Let R_j be the range measurement, and ϕ_j be a rough estimate of the bearing to the target. Then the range measurement is roughly equivalent to a LOB going through the point (R_j, ϕ_j) in direction $\phi_j + \pi/2$, and may be processed as such. ϕ_j must be estimated from other measurements or previous knowledge to within a few degrees.

8.5. Tracking

If the target is known to be stationary, then there is no difference between tracking the target and localizing it. The estimate of the target's position is independent of the order in which the various measurements are made, and the time intervals between measurements do not enter the analysis. A minor modification will handle a target moving at a known velocity. However, the problem changes if there is an unpredictable component to the target's motion. Intuitively, recent measurements should influence the estimate more than old ones in such a situation.

The most pure form of random but nonetheless continuous motion is Brownian motion or <u>diffusion</u>. Such a motion is characterized by a diffusion constant D that has dimensions of area per unit time. In any time interval of length t, a diffusing target in two dimensions suffers an increment to its position that is independent of all previous increments, each component of which is independent and normal with mean zero and variance Dt. The analytical advantage in assuming diffusion is that it fits in nicely with the assumption that the target's position before the increment is itself normal. More precisely, if Σ and Σ' are the covariance matrices of the target's position before and after the increment, then

$$\Sigma' = \Sigma + DtI, \tag{8.5-1}$$

where I is a 2×2 identity matrix. The effect of the increment is to add Dt to the diagonal elements of Σ. Graphically, the passage of time has the effect of enlarging and rounding any given error ellipse, without changing its center or orientation.

Since LOB calculations are most easily carried out in the a, b, h, f, g system, it is necessary to show how the primed quantities (after the time increment) can be obtained from the unprimed quantities. Since

$$\left(\Sigma'\right)^{-1} = \begin{pmatrix} a' & h' \\ h' & b' \end{pmatrix},$$

a', b', and h' can be obtained from 8.5-1. Since we must have $(x',y') = (x,y)$, it is clear from 8.2-2 that

$$f' = a'x + h'y$$
$$g' = h'x + b'y, \tag{8.5-2}$$

which can be solved for f and g. For example, suppose that $Dt = 2$ at a time t after the calculations associated with Figure 8-8. Since $(a, b, h) =$ $(.5, 2.5, -.5)$,

$$\begin{pmatrix} a' & h' \\ h' & b' \end{pmatrix}^{-1} = \Sigma' = \Sigma + 2I = \begin{pmatrix} .5 & -.5 \\ -.5 & 2.5 \end{pmatrix}^{-1} + \begin{pmatrix} 2 & 0 \\ 0 & 2 \end{pmatrix} = \begin{pmatrix} 4.5 & .5 \\ .5 & 2.5 \end{pmatrix}. \tag{8.5-3}$$

Invert the last matrix to obtain $(a',b',h') = (.227, .409, -.045)$. Since $(x,y) =$ $(-2.00, 2.00)$, $(f', g') = (-.544, .908)$. The primed numbers correspond to an ellipse at the same location and inclination as the one in Figure 8-8, but with $s_1' = \sqrt{s_1^2 + 2} = 2.15$ and $s_2' = \sqrt{s_2^2 + 2} = 1.54$. If now a new (θ,d,σ) LOB were obtained, we would "update" (a', b', h', f', g') by adding $\sin^2\theta/\sigma^2$ to a', $\cos^2\theta/\sigma^2$ to b', etc., in the manner of 8.2-2. These numbers would correspond to yet another ellipse. At all times the ellipse represents a complete summary of all information received to date about the target's position.

The effect of the passage of time is to enlarge the error ellipse, whereas the effect of bearing measurements is to shrink it. This encapsulates in a precise way the intuitive idea that accurate tracking of a target whose motion is not predictable requires measurements that are frequent, as well as accurate.

8.6. Kalman Filtering and Generalizations

Kalman Filtering deals with the estimation of a state vector from noisy (inaccurate) measurements when the state vector itself is changing with time. The mathematics in Section 8.3 (which dealt with noisy measurements) and in Section 8.5 (which dealt with random changes in the state vector) is a special case of Kalman Filtering. Considerable generalization is possible. The state vector is not required to be two-dimensional—it could, for example, be the six numbers required to express position and velocity in three dimensions. The measurement can be a scalar or a vector of different dimension than the state vector, and could include the time rate of change of the range to the target (typically obtained from a Doppler shift) among its components. In fact, sufficient latitude is available that the theory is applicable to practically any tracking problem. Whether it should be applied depends on how closely the assumptions required by the theory are satisfied in practice. In particular, Kalman Filter theory [2,3] assumes that

a) Measurements are linear functions of the state vector.

b) Measurement errors are normal.

Each of these assumptions is discussed below.

Assumption a) is usually not satisfied in tracking problems. For example, bearing as a function of two-dimensional position is arctan (Y/X), which is not a linear function of X or Y. The simplest solution to this problem is to use a linear approximation to the non-linear function that is accurate in the vicinity of a guess at the state vector. This was done implicitly in Section 8.3; it was this approximation that was responsible for the caution that bearing measurement errors had to be small. The technique is usually referred to as Extended Kalman Filtering. Extended

Kalman Filters are rather like the little girl who "when she was good she was very, very good, but when she was bad she was horrid". As long as the non-linear function is well approximated, tracking will be very close and in fact as close as possible in a least squares sense. However, once the linear approximation becomes bad, it may become even worse as successive measurements are processed, leading eventually to complete loss of track. Successful Kalman Filter based tracking algorithms generally incorporate a procedure for recognizing when this has happened and then re-establishing track. At this point design becomes more art than science.

With regard to assumption b), the main source of significantly non-normal errors in tracking problems seems to be false or multiple targets; e.g., a bearing is measured, but the bearing turns out to be associated with something other than the target being tracked. Such false measurements can result in radical shifts of the estimated state vector, which in turn can result in loss of track along the lines described above. As long as false measurements are rare, they can be handled by ignoring measurements that depart from expectations by an amount that exceeds some threshold.

Kalman filtering achieves its efficiency by assuming that the state of the target is at all times normally distributed. This makes it possible to manipulate only a mean and a covariance matrix, rather than an entire probability distribution over multiple dimensions of state space. When the normality assumption becomes untenable, it becomes tempting to sacrifice efficiency and track the entire probability distribution. This tactic is already being employed, and will become more attractive as computer speed and memory continue to increase. See Reference [4].

CHAPTER 8. <u>Exercises</u>

1. Demonstrate graphically the claim that RRR and LLL are the only two cases where the target lies within the cocked hat (Section 8.1). Remember that the position of the target and the directions of the lines are arbitrary but fixed in all eight cases.

2. Figure 8-16 shows a localization problem in the top part, with a 10× blow-up of the cocked hat in the bottom part. The three observers have angular error standard deviations $(w_1, w_2, w_3) = (.025, .02, .015)$ radians. Verify that the one sigma error ellipse shown in the bottom is correct. Hint: Choose the origin of coordinates near the cocked hat in the bottom part, and utilize sheet "Dir Find" of *Search4.xls* if available.

    ANSWER: By measurement, $(r_1, r_2, r_3) = (123, 137, 127)$ (miles) and $(\theta_1, \theta_2, \theta_3) = (.262, -.340, -.667)$ (radians). Therefore $(a, b, h) = (.1274, .3873, .1494)$ (miles)$^{-2}$, $\theta = -.43$ radians, and $(s_1, s_2) = (4.1, 1.5)$ miles. The values for f, g, x, and y depend on the coordinate system chosen; for the system with origin X in Figure 8-16, $(d_1, d_2, d_3) = (.4, -1.4, .6)$; $(f, g) = (.029, .005)$; and $(x, y) = (.446, -.185)$. Note that (x, y) is not the center of gravity of the cocked hat.

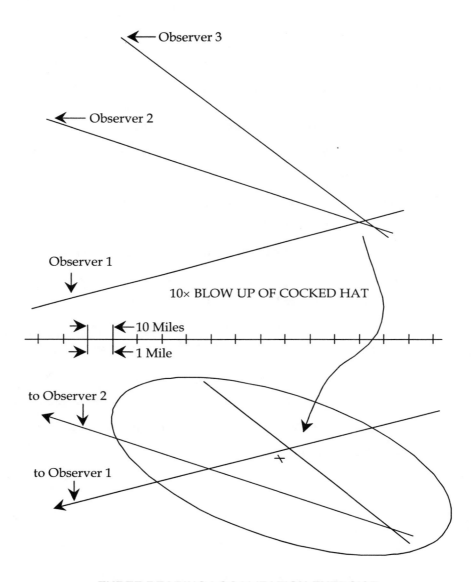

Observer 3

Observer 2

Observer 1

10× BLOW UP OF COCKED HAT

10 Miles

1 Mile

to Observer 2

to Observer 1

THREE BEARING LOCALIZATION EXERCISE

3. Verify that the product $s_1 s_2$ from Exercise 2 could have been obtained directly from 8.3-4.

4. Repeat Exercise 2 except that each r_j is decreased by a factor of 10 and each w_j is increased by a factor of 10.

   ANSWER. Formally, the solution is the same as Exercise 2. However, the angular errors are now so large that the accuracy of the solution is doubtful.

5. If the diffusion constant D is .5 (miles^2/minute) in Exercise 2, what would the area of the two sigma ellipses be one hour after the three LOB's were made?

   ANSWER: $A = 4\pi s_1' s_2' = 4\pi \sqrt{\left(s_1^2 + 30\right)\left(s_2^2 + 30\right)} = 488$ (miles^2)

REFERENCES

[1] Daniels, H. 1951. The theory of position finding. *J. Royal Stat. Soc.* (B), **13** 186–199.

[2] Gelb, A. 1974. Applied optimal estimation. MIT Press, Cambridge, MA.

[3] Jazwinski, A. 1970. *Stochastic Processes and Filtering Theory.* Academic Press, New York.

[4] Stone, L., C. Barlow, T. Corwin. 1999. *Bayesian Multiple Target Tracking.* Artech House, Boston.

9. MULTIPLE TARGETS

Some of the material developed in earlier chapters for a single target is also applicable when there are many targets. If many targets are located independently with a common probability density, for example, then the distribution of effort that maximizes detection probability for any given target will also maximize the average number of targets detected. In some cases, however, the presence of multiple targets leads to an essentially different type of problem. Some of these problems will be considered in this chapter, supposing in all cases that the targets are located randomly in the manner discussed in the next section.

9.1. Poisson Fields

Basic to the models in this chapter is the idea of a two-dimensional field of targets all located at random, subject only to the constraint that the average number of targets per unit area should be d, the target density. More precisely, we assume that every small region of area a contains a target with probability da, with a negligible probability of more than one target if a is sufficiently small, and that the numbers of targets in non-overlapping regions are independent random variables. Let A be the area of a region within the field that is not necessarily small, and let N_A be the number of targets in it. By partitioning A into a large number K of small regions of area A/K and invoking independence, we have

$$P(N_A = 0) = \lim_{k \to \infty} \left(1 - d\frac{A}{K}\right)^K = e^{-dA},$$

since each of the K subregions must not contain a target if $N_A = 0$. More generally,

$$P(N_A = n) = \frac{(dA)^n}{n!} e^{-dA}, \quad n = 0,1,2,\dots, \tag{9.1-1}$$

which is a Poisson distribution, hence the name "Poisson field".

The reader who is familiar with the Poisson process will recognize the Poisson field as a two-dimensional generalization. One major difference is that the idea of "the next target" is perforce missing in two dimensions, since two-dimensional points cannot be ordered in the same way that real numbers can. However, each point in two dimensions still has a nearest neighboring target. Let P be any point (P may or may not represent a target), and let R be the distance to the nearest neighbor. Let N_r be the number of targets within r of P. Then, since the events $R > r$ and $N_r = 0$ are the same, and since the area of a circle with radius r is πr^2,

$$P(R > r) = P(N_r = 0) = \exp(-d\pi r^2). \tag{9.1-2}$$

This may be clearer upon inspecting Figure 9-2, which illustrates a sample in a rectangle of a Poisson field with density $d = 5.2$/unit area. The figure was generated by first drawing a circle of radius $r = .2$ around P, then

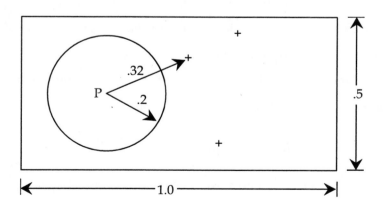

SAMPLE OF A POISSON FIELD IN A RECTANGLE

sampling the Poisson distribution with mean 2.6 (the sample was three targets), and then locating the three targets uniformly and independently at random within the rectangle. None of the three targets lies within the circle in this instance, and $R = .32$. With sufficient patience one could measure $P(R > .2)$ by generating several thousand samples of the Poisson field in this manner, but this is unnecessary because of the closed form expression 9.1-2, from which $P(R > .2) = .52$. Formula 9.1-2 is the probability law for the random variable R, from which all moments can be derived. For example,

$$\text{(see Exercise 6)} \qquad E(R) = \int_0^\infty P(R > r)dr = \left(2\sqrt{d}\right)^{-1}. \qquad (9.1\text{-}3)$$

An important characteristic of a Poisson field is that the target positions are uniformly and independently distributed within any bounded area, given the number of targets in the area. This property was exploited in constructing Figure 9-2, and is generally of use in efficiently simulating Poisson fields. Samples of a Poisson field with density d inside any bounded region S may be obtained by first inscribing S in a rectangle, then obtaining a sample with density d within the rectangle (as in Figure 9-2), and then finally erasing the part of the rectangle (including the targets in it) that does not belong to S.

9.2. Sweeping a Poisson Field

Consider a searcher with speed V and lateral range curve $p(x)$ who travels a straight line through an infinite Poisson field with density d. It is convenient to imagine a reference axis perpendicular to the searcher's track, moving along with the searcher, along which lateral range x can be measured. The rate at which targets pass through a small interval dx along this axis is $Vd\ dx$ on the average, since in time dt all targets in an area of size $(V\,dt)\,(dx)$ pass through. Each of these targets is detected with probability $p(x)$, so the total rate of detecting targets is $\int_{-\infty}^{\infty} Vd\,p(x)dx$. But this is just VdW, by definition of sweepwidth W. Thus, a sensor is completely characterized by its sweepwidth for purposes of sweeping a Poisson field.

The above simple result does not hold in sweeping a "lattice" where a target is located at each corner in a grid of squares with side $1/\sqrt{d}$. In that case, the rate of detecting targets can be quite sensitive to the orientation of the searcher's track. This is an instance of the remarkably common result that the assumption of randomness leads to essentially simpler results than the assumption of regularity. The basic reason is that random structures have fewer "properties" than regular structures. It is impossible to orient oneself in a Poisson field, for example, since all directions are equivalent.

9.3. Mean Free Paths

How far will a marble of diameter W roll in a Poisson field with density d before it (more precisely, its shadow) encounters a target? Equivalently, how far will a searcher who sees all targets within $W/2$ proceed before seeing a target? The answer is a simple consequence of 9.1-1. Let the searcher be placed anywhere in the field, and ignore immediate detections of targets that are within $W/2$ of the initial position. After moving a distance x, the searcher has covered an area Wx. Let N_x be the number of targets in the area, and let X be the distance to the first target (the free path). Then the events $(N_x = 0)$ and $(X > x)$ are the same, so

$$P(X > x) = P(N_x = 0) = \exp(-Wdx),$$

according to 9.1-1. So X is an exponential random variable and the mean free path is $E(X) = (dW)^{-1}$.

9.4. Exhaustive Inspection

Consider a searcher who must actually visit every target in a large but finite Poisson field with density d, and assume he can detect all targets within $W/2$, the cookie-cutter detection law. The visit is required because the targets must be gathered or identified as well as detected. The problem is to search in such a manner that the total track length required to visit all targets is minimized.

One method of exhaustively searching the field is shown in Figure 9-6. The idea is to sweep out channels of width W, making excursions from the baseline track to visit each target. The average length of an excursion (going out and coming back) is $W/2$. The average length of travel required to sweep out a baseline of length L is therefore $L + (WLd) (W/2)$, since WLd targets, on the average, will have to be visited. The amount of travel required per unit area swept is therefore

$$z = 1/W + dW/2. \qquad (9.4\text{-}1)$$

It is of interest that z is not minimized by making $W = \infty$. It is possible that a target might be detected so far away that visitation should be deferred to a subsequent sweep.

The method of searching outlined above is simple and reasonably effective, but is almost certainly not optimal. When W is infinite, the problem is essentially a travelling salesman problem [3], which is known to be difficult, and the inclusion of a finite W presumably does not make determination of an optimal strategy any easier. However, it seems clear that the optimal strategy should be more opportunistic than the one analyzed above. For example, target c could have been visited very

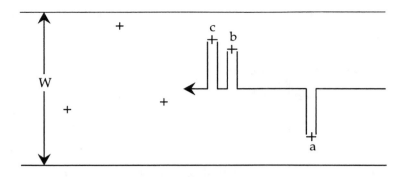

ILLUSTRATION OF EXHAUSTIVE SEARCH WITH VISITATION IN A POISSON FIELD

cheaply when the searcher was at target b in Figure 9-6, even if the searcher subsequently had to return to target b in order to keep his pattern intact. There has apparently been very little experimentation along these lines with the goal of finding an improved (more visits per unit time) exhaustive inspection strategy. In the sense of that metric, the most efficient strategy would permit a small probability of not visiting a target; that is, it would not be exhaustive. Reiss [2] describes the results of some simulation experiments that illuminate the tradeoff between exhaustiveness and efficiency.

9.5. Finding a Particular Target

Suppose that the position of a "true" target is known to within a circular normal error with standard deviation σ, and that the problem of finding it is complicated by the fact that it is indistinguishable from any of the "false" targets that surround it in a Poisson field with density d. Assume further that search consists of the examination of a circular region of radius r centered on the estimated true target position, with the method of search being such that a target is selected at random if there is more than one target in the region. The object is to determine the value of r that makes the probability of detecting the true target as large as possible.

Let D be the event that the true target is detected, let E be the event that the true target is within the circle, and let N_r be the number of false targets in the circle. Then $P(D \mid E$ and $(N_r = n)) = 1/(n + 1)$, and (from Section 1.4) $P(E) = 1 - \exp(-r^2/2\sigma^2)$. Since N_r is Poisson with mean $d\pi r^2 \equiv z$,

$$P(D) = \sum_{n=0}^{\infty} P(D \mid E \text{ and } (N_r = n)) P(E) P(N_r = n)$$

$$= P(E) \sum_{n=0}^{\infty} \frac{1}{n+1} \frac{z^n}{n!} \exp(-z) \tag{9.5-1}$$

$$= P(E) \exp(-z) \left(\sum_{n=0}^{\infty} \frac{z^{n+1}}{(n+1)!} \right) \Big/ z$$

$$= P(E) \exp(-z) (\exp(z) - 1) \big/ z$$

$$= \left(1 - \exp\left(-r^2/2\sigma^2\right) \right) (1 - \exp(-z)) \big/ z.$$

Let $K = 2\pi d\sigma^2$. Then $r^2/2\sigma^2 = z/K$, and

$$P(D) = (1 - \exp(-z/K))(1 - \exp(-z)) \big/ z. \tag{9.5-2}$$

Selecting r to maximize $P(D)$ is the same as selecting the dimensionless number z. Let $z(K)$ be the maximizing value for z, and let $p(K)$ be the maximum value of $P(D)$. There is no closed form expression for $z(K)$, but $z(K)$ and $p(K)$ are both graphed in Figure 9-9. The fact that $p(K)$ is considerably less than 1.0 unless K is very small is noteworthy; even a small false target density is a considerable handicap in finding the true target. The function $z(K)$ can be accurately approximated when K is either large or small by

$$z(K) \approx \begin{cases} K\ell n(2/K) & \text{for } K \leq .2 \\ \ell n(2K) & \text{for } K \geq 5. \end{cases} \qquad (9.5\text{-}3)$$

For example, suppose $\sigma = 1$ mile and $d = .1$ false targets per square mile. Then $K = .628$, $z(K) = .99$, and $p(K) = .5$. The optimal value of r is $\sqrt{2\sigma^2 z(K)/K} = 1.8$ miles. If instead $d = .01$ false targets per square mile, then $K = .0628$, $z(K) = .22$ (from 9.5-3), $p(K) = .87$, and the optimal value of r is 2.6 miles.

The above analysis assumes that the search is exhaustive—all targets (true or false) within r of the origin are detected. Kalbaugh [1] bases his analysis instead on the random search assumption, finding the distribution of effort that maximizes the probability of finding the true target.

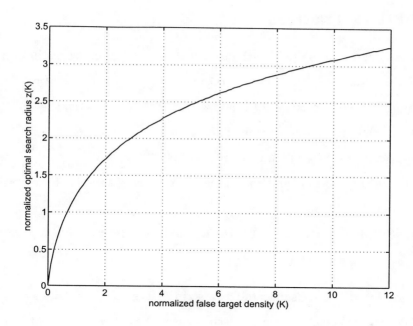

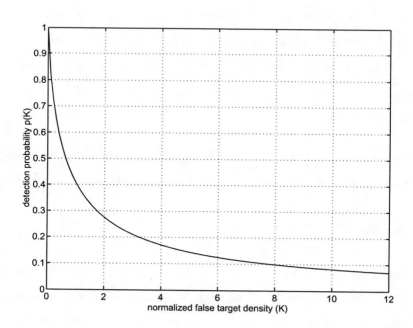

ILLUSTRATING THE FUNCTIONS *z(K)* AND *p(K)*.

CHAPTER 9. Exercises

1. Consider a Poisson field with density .9 targets per unit area in a circle with radius 1.

    a) If N_A is the number of targets within the circle, sketch the probability mass function of N_A.

    b) What are the mean and variance of N_A?

    c) Using a table of random numbers, construct a sample of the Poisson field.

    ANSWER: $dA = 2.83$, 9.1-1 is the probability mass function, and $E(N_A) = \text{Var}(N_A) = 2.83$.

2. Two territories are separated by a strip that is infinitely long and 100 meters deep. Within the strip, sensors have been placed at random (i.e., in a Poisson field) with density .001 sensors per square meter. Each sensor will detect any penetrator who comes within 10 meters of it. What is the probability that a penetrator who travels from one territory to the other will not be detected by any sensor?

    ANSWER: .135.

3. In exhaustive search of a Poisson field, what sweepwidth minimizes z in 9.4-1? For this sweepwidth, what fraction of the searcher's time is spent traveling the baseline?

    ANSWER $W = \sqrt{2/d}$, .5.

4. Suppose that search is conducted in the manner of Section 9.5 when $\sigma = 200$ meters and $d = 10$ false targets per square kilometer. What region should be searched, what is the probability that the true target is within the region, and what is $P(D)$?

ANSWER: A circle centered on the estimated target position with radius 246 meters should be searched, and $P(D) = .24$. The probability that the true target is within the circle is .53.

5. A different search plan than the one outlined in Section 9.5 would be to start at the estimated true target position and spiral outward until a target is encountered. If this is feasible, it will give a higher probability of detecting the true target. Let R_T and R_F be the radial distances to the true target and the nearest false target, respectively. Then R_T and R_F are independent random variables, and the probability of detecting the true target is just $P(D) = P(R_T < R_F)$.

   a) Derive an analytic expression for $P(D)$, utilizing the fact that the probability laws for R_T and R_F are known.

   b) Compare this method with the method outlined in 9.5 by sketching the answer to a) on Figure 9-9.

   ANSWER: $P(D) = (1 + 2\pi d\sigma^2)^{-1} = (1 + K)^{-1}$.

6. Justify the two equalities in 9.1-3.

7. In Section 9.3, what would the mean free path have been if immediate detections of targets within $W/2$ were counted, with the associated free path being zero in that case?

   ANSWER: $E(D) = \exp(-d\pi W^2/4)/(dW)$.

REFERENCES

[1]   Kalbaugh, D. 1993. Search density for a stationary target. *Oper. Res.* **41** 310–318.

[2]   Reiss, M. 1980. *On the Optimization of a Search Pattern for Maritime Surveillance, in Search Theory and Applications.* K. B. Haley and L. D. Stone, eds. Plenum Press, NATO Conference Series, New York, 141–153.

[3]   Winston, W. 1994. *Operations Research: Applications and Algorithms*, Wadsworth.

10. FALSE ALARMS AND FALSE TARGETS

In any detection system, there must be a decision-making stage in which the "target" or "no target" decision is made, based on certain physical measurements. It is inevitable that there must arise circumstances where the issue is in doubt, so that the possibility of a false alarm arises. Let p_f be the false alarm probability (probability of a target call given that no target is present) and p_d be the detection probability (the probability of a target call given that a target is present). The decision-making stage must make a compromise between p_f and p_d. A conservative decision criterion will make p_f low at the cost of also making p_d low, whereas an aggressive criterion will make p_d high at the expense of making p_f high. The probability of detection can always be increased if the associated increase in false alarms is acceptable.

Given the inevitable tradeoff between p_d and p_f, any attempt to derive or measure p_d without some sort of control on p_f is in theory meaningless, and is in practice subject to non-repeatability of the experiment that measures p_d. This fact has been a continuing difficulty for human factors researchers attempting to measure human responses to stimuli in the tradition of Fechner [2]. A subject who is attempting to demonstrate that he can detect very small stimulus differences will have a higher detection probability than a subject whose main objective is to avoid the embarrassment associated with claiming that he can tell the difference between two identical stimuli.

Since World War II, when the required theory was developed by radar workers, there has been a tendency to measure a Receiver Operating Characteristic (ROC) curve that shows the tradeoff between p_d and p_f, rather than to simply measure p_d [6]. In many circumstances, the ROC curve is a member of a class that is characterized by a single parameter called the detection index (d). The detection index is a dimensionless measure of sensitivity that has proved to possess the stability properties under repeated measurement that p_d lacks. Sections 10.1 through 10.4 deal with this view of the false alarm problem. Sections 10.5 and 10.6 take an essentially different view where false targets can be exposed as such if the required effort is spent on classification.

10.1. Single Look for a Known Signal in Additive Gaussian Noise

Automatic detection devices such as sonar and radar often make the detection decision based on the magnitude of a voltage V; for some threshold level v, a detection is electronically called if and only if $V \geq v$. Let s be the known component of V that is due to the target. The presence of electrical noise has the effect of adding a random noise N to s, so that

$$V = s + N \quad \text{when a target is present, or} \qquad (10.1\text{-}1)$$

$$V = N \qquad \text{when no target is present.} \qquad (10.1\text{-}2)$$

If there were no noise, it would be possible to avoid false alarms while assuring detections by setting the threshold v to be any value between zero and s. The presence of the noise term, however, invariably results in the possibility that noise alone will exceed the threshold. The situation is illustrated in Figure 10-3, which shows two probability density functions—the one on the left for noise alone and the one on the right for signal plus noise. p_f and p_d are indicated as shaded areas for a particular value of v. By considering various values for v, one can show the corresponding pairs (p_d, p_f) as an ROC curve, generally with p_d shown as a function of p_f. Figure 10-4 shows several examples.

10-2

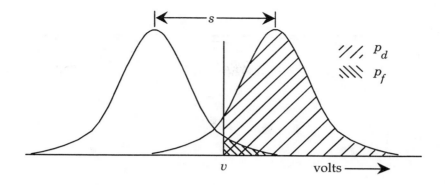

DISTRIBUTION OF THE VOLTAGE WITH AND WITHOUT A SIGNAL

In the event that the noise is normally distributed with mean μ and variance σ^2, then

$$p_f = 1 - \Phi\left(\frac{v - \mu}{\sigma}\right)$$

$$p_d = 1 - \Phi\left(\frac{v - \mu - s}{\sigma}\right),$$

(10.1-3)

where Φ is the cumulative normal function. Equation 10.1-3 can also be written

$$p_f = 1 - \Phi(x)$$

$$p_d = 1 - \Phi(x - \sqrt{d}), \quad \text{where}$$

$$x \equiv (v - \mu)/\sigma$$

$$d \equiv s^2/\sigma^2 = \text{"detection index"}.$$

(10.1-4)

In 10.1-4, x is a dimensionless threshold, and d is a dimensionless measure of the separation of the two density functions shown in Figure 10-3. By varying x, an ROC curve can be generated for every value of d. Figure 10-4 shows several such ROC curves with d as a parameter.

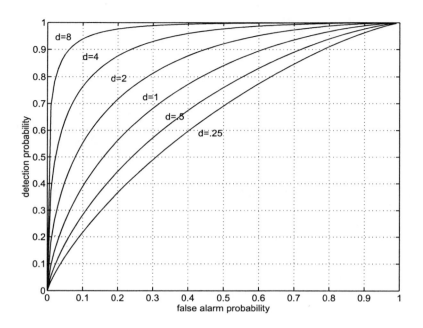

RECEIVER OPERATING CHARACTERISTIC (ROC) CURVES

In radar, all field strengths are proportional to the square root of the amount of power generated, and therefore so is the voltage s, even though the received signal may be linearly processed in various ways before the threshold test is made. Therefore, s^2 is proportional to power generated. Also, σ^2 is proportional to the average amount of noise power, so the detection index d is proportional to the ratio of signal power to noise power. The same conclusion follows for sonar if "pressure" is substituted for "field strength" in the above. Thus, d can generally be interpreted as a signal to noise power ratio. Since power is a fundamental quantity, this interpretation is useful. In passive detection systems that receive power radiated from the target after it has been dissipated by spherical spreading, for example, power received is proportional to R^{-2}, where R is range. Thus, halving the range has the effect of quadrupling the detection index. Active systems encounter the dissipation twice, so that halving the range has the effect of multiplying the detection index by 16.

The virtue of the above theory for human detection problems is not that it permits an explicit computation of d, but rather that it provides a reasonable one parameter class of ROC curves. The extent to which theory fits experiment is discussed in [6].

10.2. Multiple Looks for a Known Signal

When the signal is known, it can be made to stand out from the noise by averaging n independent measurements V_1, ..., V_n. Let $V = (V_1 + ... + V_n)/n$. If a target is present, then the expected value of V is $E(V | \text{target present}) = s + \mu$; otherwise, $E(V | \text{no target}) = \mu$. In either case, the variance of V is σ^2/n. Averaging leaves the mean unchanged and reduces the variance. From 10.1-4, the detection index is now

$$d = \frac{[(s+\mu) - \mu]^2}{(\sigma^2/n)} = n(s^2/\sigma^2); \qquad (10.2\text{-}1)$$

i.e., the effect of averaging n independent measurements is to increase d by the factor n.

It was implicitly assumed above that the noise-free signal s does not vary over the averaging period. The analysis can be generalized to deal with index-dependent values s_1, ..., s_n if s^2 in 10.2-1 is changed to $\left(s_1^2 + ... + s_n^2\right)/n \equiv$ average signal power. The assumption that s_1, ..., s_n are known quantities is essential, but they do not have to all be the same.

Averaging is carried out by electronic integration over some time period t. Let τ be a "coherence time" for the type of noise present; the idea is that noise voltages separated by τ from each other in time can be assumed to be independent. Then averaging over a period t is statistically equivalent to averaging $n = t/\tau$ independent samples, so

$$d = (t/\tau)\left(s^2/\sigma^2\right). \tag{10.2-2}$$

Note that the detection index is proportional to time and power (i.e., to energy) in detecting a known signal.

The assumption that the signal is known is reasonable in active detection systems where the received echo is more or less a replica of the transmitted signal except for a time delay and a scale change. In passive systems, and sometimes even in active systems where the signal is subjected to nonlinear environmental effects, the analysis of the next section may be more appropriate. There is a great deal more to be said on this topic. The reader is referred to [7] for sonar detection or [4] for radar detection.

10.3. Multiple Looks for an Unknown Signal

An extreme case of an unknown signal is where the signal emitted by the target takes the same form as the noise. In this case, suppose

$$V_i = \begin{cases} S_i + N_i & \text{when a target is present} \\ N_i & \text{when no target is present,} \end{cases} \tag{10.3-1}$$

where S_i is the voltage due to the target and N_i is the voltage due to the noise. Assume that S_i and N_i are independent, normally distributed random variables with mean zero and variances s^2 (for S_i) and σ^2 (for N_i).

Since V_i is normal and zero on the average whether a target is present or not, decisions can not be based on the sample mean V as in 10.2. Instead, decisions should be based on the variance or power estimate $X = \left(V_1^2 + ... + V_n^2\right)/n$, concluding that a target is present when X exceeds some threshold. This is called a square law detector. Assuming that the V_i are all independent, we have

$$E(X|\text{target present}) = s^2 + \sigma^2$$

$$E(X|\text{no target present}) = \sigma^2$$

$$\text{Var}(X|\text{target present}) = 2(s^4 + \sigma^4)/n$$

(10.3-2)

$$\text{Var}(X|\text{no target present}) = 2\sigma^4/n.$$

Formulas 10.3-2 follow from the fact that X is a Chi-square random variable. Since the variance of X depends on whether a target is present, the ROC curve is not in general a member of the class introduced in Section 10.1; that is, a detection index does not exist in general. However, for weak signals where s is small compared to σ and n is large, the two variance expressions in 10.3-2 are nearly equal and X is nearly normal by the Central Limit Theorem, so

$$d = \frac{\left[(s^2 + \sigma^2) - \sigma^2\right]^2}{\left[2\sigma^4/n\right]} = (n/2)(s^4/\sigma^4).$$

(10.3-3)

As in Section 10.2, if t and τ are respectively the integration time and the coherence time, n can be replaced by t/τ. Note that the detection index is now proportional to the square of power, since s^2 is proportional to power. Since d is only linearly proportional to integration time, it is more important to have a strong signal than a long time to examine it when the form of the signal is unknown; this can be contrasted with 10.2-2, where time and power are of equal importance.

Formula 10.3-3 is only valid for weak signals. A reasonable constraint on its use is $s \le \sigma$. Note that d as computed from 10.3-3 is smaller than d as computed from 10.2-1 over this range. This is natural, since surely nothing can be gained by being ignorant of the signal.

10.4. Optimization of the Detection Threshold

In principle, the detection threshold can be set optimally if the "costs" associated with false alarms and missed detections are both known. Specifically, let

c_1 = cost of a missed detection

c_2 = cost of a false alarm

p = (unconditional) probability that a target is present on any given look

$q = 1 - p$

c = average cost per look.

Then,

$$c = pc_1(1 - p_d) + qc_2p_f. \tag{10.4-1}$$

The threshold affects both p_d and p_f, and should be set to minimize c. If p_d and p_f are linked by 10.1-4, then the minimization can be accomplished through differentiation (Exercise 4), but the principle is the same in any case: set the threshold to minimize c. Alternatively, the principle is to set p_f to minimize c, since p_d depends implicitly on p_f.

In practice, the consequences of the two types of error are typically so disparate that it is difficult to measure c_1 and c_2 on a common scale. For this reason, the false alarm probability is typically not formally optimized in practice. Theoretical discussions of sensitivity in engineering journals typically show p_d as a function of signal-to-noise ratio, with p_f held constant at a level that is not defended as being anything but "reasonable". For a pulsed radar, for example, p_f will typically be held constant at 10^{-5} or 10^{-6}. Such numbers may seem at first sight to be so small as to be negligible, but they are not. If the radar emits 1000 pulses per second, and if each pulse requires a technical decision for each of 1000 distinct ranges, then the false alarm rate when $p_f = 10^{-6}$ is 1/second. In general, the false alarm rate is p_f/δ where δ is the time between technical decisions. When δ is very small, p_f must also be very small, since it is the ratio p_f/δ that is of operational significance.

If there are actually many targets, with the objective being to detect them at as great a rate as possible, then it is natural to set the false alarm probability to maximize the detection rate. Suppose, for example, that each detection opportunity requires a technical decision (which takes a time δ, plus a relatively lengthy investigation of length τ in the event that the technical decision is to call a target. As long as no target is present, the average time required per detection opportunity is $\delta + \tau p_f$. If a target is present every $(n+1)$ opportunities, then the average rate at which targets are detected (neglecting the time required to actually inspect the target) is

$$r_d = \frac{p_d}{n(\delta + \tau p_f)} = \frac{1}{n\delta}\frac{p_d}{1+(\tau/\delta)p_f}. \tag{10.4-2}$$

The "optimal" false alarm probability will maximize the effective detection rate r_d. If p_d and p_f are linked by 10.1-4, then the optimal p_f depends on the detection index d and the dimensionless ratio τ/δ (see Exercise 5).

In many cases the sweepwidth W is a better measure of performance than p_d, since the signal voltage s depends on how far away the target is. If τ has the same meaning as above, and if $f \equiv p_f/\delta$ is the false alarm rate, then Pollock [3] has shown that $W' = W/(1 + f\tau)$ is an equivalent "no false alarm" sweepwidth for random searches. W and f each depend on the threshold, which should be set to maximize W'.

10.5. Optimal Search in the Presence of False Targets

This section considers a distribution of effort problem of the type encountered in Section 5.2, except that cell i now has δ_i false targets in it, on the average. The false targets are assumed to be physical objects that must be classified immediately upon discovery, after which each is marked so that repeated examination of the same false target is not necessary. This feature means that one cannot proceed by defining an equivalent sweepwidth as in Section 10.4, but must take an essentially different view of the problem [5].

The natural optimization problem to consider would be maximization of the probability of detecting the true target before some fixed time. Unfortunately, that problem is too difficult, with the difficulty being directly traceable to the fact that discovery of a false target provides information, but does not terminate the search. Instead, consider maximizing the probability of detection subject to a constraint on the average amount of time spent searching and classifying false targets, but not including the amount of time required to classify the true target. This seemingly minor change in the meaning of the constraint is actually a major mathematical advantage when coupled with the final assumption that the class of search plans under investigation is <u>non-adaptive</u>. A non-adaptive plan is simply a vector $\underline{x} = (t_1, \ldots, t_n)$, where t_i is the amount of time spent searching in cell i regardless of how many false targets are discovered there. The total amount of search time $t = \Sigma t_i$ is therefore deterministic, although the total amount of time spent classifying whatever false targets are discovered is random. If the average of this latter quantity is u, then $\underline{x}$ must be such that $t + u$ meets a constraint.

Within that constraint, the probability of detecting the true target is to be maximized.

Define the following:

n = number of cells

δ_i = average number of false targets in cell i

τ_i = average classification time for a false target in cell i

p_i = probability the true target is in cell i

t_i = search time in cell i (non-negative)

$b_i(t_i)$ = probability of detecting any given target in cell i

$f(\underline{x})$ = probability of detection = $\Sigma p_i b_i(t_i)$

t = search time = Σt_i

u = average false target classification time = $\Sigma \delta_i \tau_i b_i(t_i)$

$g(\underline{x})$ = total average time = $t + u$.

The objective is to maximize $f(\underline{x})$ subject to a constraint on $g(\underline{x})$. With the intent of finally applying Everett's Theorem (Section 5.1), instead maximize the Lagrangian $f(\underline{x}) - \lambda g(\underline{x})$. Since $f(\underline{x}) - \lambda g(\underline{x})$ is a sum of functions of one variable, the maximization over $\underline{x}$ is equivalent to the relatively simple problem of performing n single variable maximizations. Define $t_i(\lambda)$ as follows:

$$t_i(\lambda) \text{ maximizes } p_i b_i(t_i) - \lambda(t_i + \delta_I \tau_i b_i(t_i)) \qquad (10.5\text{-}1)$$

$$\text{subject to } t_i \geq 0.$$

The maximizing value $t_i(\lambda)$ in 10.5-1 will typically but not necessarily be unique, and in any case can be taken to be a finite, decreasing function of λ for $\lambda > 0$. Let $\underline{x}(\lambda) = (t_1(\lambda), ..., t_n(\lambda))$. Then Everett's Theorem states that the maximum value of $f(\underline{x})$, subject to the constraint $g(\underline{x}) \leq g(\underline{x}(\lambda))$, is $f(\underline{x}(\lambda))$.

The problem has been reduced to searching for the value of λ for which $g(\underline{x}(\lambda))$ is the constraint on total average time.

Example.

$\underline{p} = (1/3,\ 1/3,\ 1/3)$, $\underline{\delta} = (1.5,\ 1.5,\ 2)$, $\underline{\tau} = (2/3,\ 2/3,\ 1)$,

$b_i(t_i) = 1 - \exp(-\alpha_i t_i)$, $\underline{\alpha} = (1,\ 2,\ 3)$. In this example, the second cell is easier to search than the first $(\alpha_2 > \alpha_1)$, and the third cell is easier yet but has lots of false targets that are difficult to classify. The maximization can be accomplished by equating the derivative of $p_i b_i(t_i) - \lambda(t_i + \delta_I \tau_i b_i(t_i))$ to zero and solving for $t_i(\lambda)$, except that $t_i(\lambda)$ is taken to be zero if the calculation results in a negative number:

$$t_i(\lambda) = \left\{ \frac{1}{\alpha_i} \ln\left(\alpha_i p_i / \lambda - \alpha_i \delta_i \tau_i \right) \right\}^+ , \tag{10.5-2}$$

where the + superscript ensures $t_i(\lambda) \geq 0$. Table 10-12 shows the results for several arbitrarily chosen values of λ.

λ	t_1	t_2	t_3	t	u	f
.01	3.47	2.09	1.53	7.09	3.93	.98
.1	.85	.87	.69	2.41	3.14	.47
.2	0	.42	.37	.79	1.90	.41
.3	0	.10	.10	.20	.68	.21
.4	0	0	0	0	0	0

DISTRIBUTION OF EFFORT FOR VARIOUS λ

According to the fourth row of Table 10-12, for example, if a total of .20 + .68 = .88 units of time are available for search and false target classification, and if a non-adaptive search plan is desired, then the best non-adaptive plan is to ignore the first cell and search for .1 time units in each of the other two. An average of .68 time units is required to classify all the false targets encountered, and the probability of detecting the true target is .21. Note that large detection probabilities require large search times, but that the average classification time never exceeds $\Sigma \delta_I \tau_i = 4$ time units for any λ.

The functions $t_i(\lambda)$ are decreasing functions of λ, and therefore so is $t(\lambda) \equiv \Sigma t_i(\lambda)$. If $t(\lambda)$ is also a continuous function of λ, as it will certainly be if 10.5-2 holds, then it will always be possible to solve the equation $t(\lambda) = t$ for any t for which the detection probability is less than 1. This means that any amount of search time t can be optimally split into the several cells, with the amount of search time in each cell being an increasing function of t. Consider the search policy that gradually increases the amount of search time in each cell in such a manner that the total amount of search time is always divided optimally. We will refer to this policy as the ONAP (optimal non-adaptive policy). In the example, the ONAP would split the first .2 units of search time (0, .1, .1), the first .79 units of search time (0, .42, .37), etc. A more complete version of Table 10-12 would give a more complete description of the ONAP. The ONAP will eventually detect the true target with probability 1, if all of the functions $b_i(t_i)$ approach 1 in the limit.

Let $X(z)$ be the amount of search time plus the amount of time spent classifying false targets when the probability of detection is z. For every z, the ONAP minimizes $E(X(z))$; in the example, $E(X(.21)) \geq .88$ for all non-adaptive policies, with equality holding for the ONAP, etc. Let the random variable Z be the probability of detection as of the time when the true target is detected. Since the event $(Z \leq z)$ is just the event that the target is detected sometime before the probability of detection reaches z,

$P(Z \le z) = z$, which means that Z is uniformly distributed on [0,1]. The random variable $X(Z)$ is the total amount of time required to detect the target. By conditional expectation,

$$E(X(Z)) = \int_0^1 E(X(Z)|Z = z)dz = \int_0^1 E(X(z)|Z = z)dz . \qquad (10.5\text{-}3)$$

Assuming that the position of the target is independent of all random variables associated with false targets, $E(X(z) \mid Z = z) = E(X(z))$. Since the ONAP minimizes $E(X(z))$ for all z, it must therefore also minimize $E(X(Z))$, which quantity will be subsequently referred to as T_{ONAP}. This minimization is probably the most satisfying sense in which the ONAP is optimal, and it is on this basis that the ONAP is compared with other plans below.

The ONAP is optimal within the class of non-adaptive search plans. It would be natural to next investigate how much can be gained by permitting the search plan to be adaptive. There appears to be exactly one instance of an optimal adaptive plan that has been worked out in the literature; this is in Section 8 of Dobbie [1], where a two-cell problem with a single false target in cell 2 is worked out under the assumptions that $b_i(t_i) = 1 - \exp(-t_i)$ and that a single unit of time is required for classification. In the special case where $\underline{p}$ = (.358, .632), Dobbie's optimal adaptive plan (OAP) is as follows: Divide search effort equally between the two cells until a target is detected. If the target turns out to be false, search an additional .583 time units in cell 2, and then split search time evenly until the true target is detected. If this plan is followed, the average amount of time required to detect the target (T_{OAP}), using equation 45 of the reference, is 2.46 time units. If the ONAP is followed instead, the average amount of time required to detect the target is $T_{\text{ONAP}} = 2.47$ time units, obtained by evaluating

$$\int_0^1 E(X(z)) dz$$

numerically. The difference between the ONAP and the OAP is slight in this example.

It is also interesting to compare the ONAP with the search plan where the target detection probabilities $b_i(t_i)$ are forced to be equal in all cells at all times, which is hereby dubbed the ENAP (equalizing non-adaptive plan). Let $b(t)$ be the common value of the target detection probabilities at search time t. Since the detection probability is the same in all cells, $b(t)$ is also the (unconditional) probability of detecting the target by search time t, regardless of the target location distribution $\underline{p}$. The average amount of search time required for detection is therefore

$$\int_0^\infty (1 - b(t)) dt$$

as in 2.1-5. Furthermore, since the probability that any given false target will be detected before the true target is .5 under the ENAP, the average amount of time spent classifying false targets before the true target is detected is $.5 \Sigma \tau_i \delta_i$. Letting T_{ENAP} be the average total time required to detect the target, we have

$$T_{\text{ENAP}} = \int_0^\infty (1 - b(t)) dt + .5 \sum \delta_i \tau_i . \tag{10.5-4}$$

In Dobbie's two-cell example, the ENAP splits search time evenly between the two cells, $b(t) = 1 - \exp(-t/2)$, and $T_{\text{ENAP}} = 2 + .5 = 2.5$. Since the ENAP is a non-adaptive plan, T_{ENAP} is necessarily an upper bound on the more difficult to compute T_{ONAP}. In this example the upper bound is sharp, but there are also examples where T_{ENAP} and T_{ONAP} differ substantially.

The quantities T_{ONAP}, T_{OAP}, and T_{ENAP} do not include the time required to actually classify the target. Assuming that this amount of time is independent of the search plan, none of the above comparisons would be changed by including it.

Reference [5] includes a discussion of optimal search in the presence of false targets in continuous space, and also permits the possibility that the detection functions $b_i(t_i)$ are not the same for true and false targets.

10.6. Operational False Alarms and Cascaded Detection Systems

Most actual detection systems seem to consist of a succession of stages, with stage $n + 1$ rejecting some fraction of the target calls of stage n, and with inspection cost or time typically increasing with stage number. In animals, for example, the eye is typically capable of detecting moving things over a wide field of view (peripheral vision), but moving objects can only be classified as prey/non-prey or threat/non-threat by momentarily focussing the object onto the narrow field of view cone cells. This two-stage system is apparently more efficient than simply casting about directly with the narrow field of view cone cell system.

In many man-made detection systems, the low-numbered stages are mechanized and the high-numbered stages are humans in supervisory order. For example, consider a military system for detecting incoming hostile aircraft. The first stage may be a long range search radar. As it sweeps, noise occasionally lights up the display, causing false alarms. In accordance with the formulas discussed earlier, the operator can adjust a threshold to jointly increase or decrease p_d and p_f. If the operator sees a "pip" on one sweep, he will typically watch several successive sweeps to see if a pip occurs in the same place. If it does not, he takes no action, but he reports it as a "contact" if it does. The "contact" may be a hostile aircraft, a friendly aircraft, the moon (it has happened), or even an unlikely sequence of noise pips in the same place on the radar scope, but in any case there are fewer "contacts" than "pips". A contact may be investigated in subsequent stages by measuring its velocity or attempting to communicate with it. The last stage may involve the expensive test of launching an aircraft to investigate visually. At each stage, the surveillance task would be prohibitively time consuming or expensive were it not for the fact that previous stages have considerably reduced the number of decisions to be made. The radar may very well make 10^6 decisions per second, but subsequent stages need to deal only with a very small fraction of that number. After a contact has successfully "passed" all of the stages, some sort of action must be taken. False alarms at this point are "operational". Operational false alarms can be very expensive, possibly causing the waste of an expensive missile or even the shooting down of a non-hostile aircraft.

Figure 10-17 shows a cascaded detection system where each stage passes only a fraction of its input to the next, with the last operational stage being expensive but perfect in the sense that its output includes no false targets. Except for the last stage, each stage i has a detection index d_i and a processing cost of c_{i-1}; $i = 1, ..., n$, with c_n being the cost of the operational stage. Since all false targets are ultimately identified, the tradeoff is between the overall probability of detecting a true target and the average cost of rejecting a false target $(\bar{c})$.

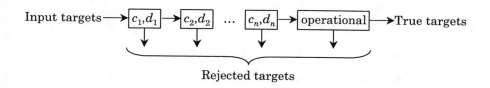

There remains the problem of setting n detection thresholds to (say) minimize $\bar{c}$ subject to a constraint that the overall detection probability must exceed a given level P_D. To illustrate the idea, we adopt the assumptions of Section 10.1 about each numbered stage. Letting x_i be the normalized detection threshold at stage i, from (10.1-4) we have

$$p_{f,i} = 1 - \Phi(x_i)$$
$$p_{d,i} = 1 - \Phi\left(x_i - \sqrt{d_i}\right)$$

(10.6-1)

Assume independence between stages, and let $q_{f,i}$ and $q_{d,i}$ be the probabilities that a false target and a true target, respectively, will pass the first i stages. Then

$$q_{f,i} = \prod_{j=1}^{i} p_{f,j}$$

$$q_{d,i} = \prod_{j=1}^{i} p_{d,j}$$

(10.6-2)

$$\bar{c} = \sum_{j=1}^{n} c_j\, q_{d,j}$$

The additive cost of the first stage c_0 has been omitted from the formula for $\bar{c}$ because it cannot be controlled. The problem is then to minimize $\bar{c}$ subject to $q_{d,n} \geq P_D$. This is the subject of sheet "Cascade" of workbook Search4.xls.

Example.

If $n = 4$, if all detection indexes and costs are 1.0, and if $P_D = .86$, the optimal x is (-.27, -.84, -1.39, -2.15) and the minimal $\bar{c}$ is 1.97. Note that the early stages are hardest to pass, since the detection thresholds decrease with stage number. This should make intuitive sense, since early rejections are cheaper than late ones. The analog of an ROC curve for this multi-stage system would be a graph of $\bar{c}$ versus P_D, one point on which is (1.97, .86).

There is a large difference between an operational false alarm and a noise false alarm of the type that causes a false pip on a radar screen. By the time a contact has survived several stages, it is likely to be a physical object or highly localized physical phenomenon of some sort, rather than an unfortunate sequence of noise pips. In this sense, the distribution of objects that can be confused with the target is of more operational importance than the amount of noise that is input to the radar. Assuming that the objects are randomly distributed in space leads to the models of Chapter 9.

The fact that operational false alarms are typically due to objects resembling the target rather than to random electrical disturbances perhaps explains why the seemingly inevitable tradeoff between p_d and p_f has actually played only a minor role in applying search theory. There is also the following consideration: Search is usually conducted by parties either desirous of approaching the sought object or of avoiding it. An approacher may suffer momentary confusion as to whether a target call actually represents a target or not, but he can resolve the confusion by beginning the natural approaching action. If the target call turns out not to be a target, then the approacher's investment is slight, and he may consequently perceive that false alarms simply do not happen in an operational sense. This argument does not work for avoiders, of course, since an avoider has a conflict between the avoidance action and the confusion resolving action. But there seem to be more approachers than avoiders in search problems.

CHAPTER 10. Exercises

1. Using Figure 10-4, graphically find the false alarm probability that minimizes the sum $2p_f + 4(1 - p_d)$ when $d = 1$. Note that this expression is of the form 10.4-1.

    ANSWER: The exact answer is $p_f = .58$, with the associated p_d being .88. The graphical answer is obtained by finding the point where the ROC curve for $d = 1$ has slope .5.

2. A given detector has a detection index of 1 and a false alarm probability of .1.

    a) What is the detection probability?

    b) What would the detection probability be if the integration time were quadrupled and the threshold were adjusted so that the false alarm probability remained .1?

    ANSWER: .39, .76. Detection index is proportional to integration time whether the signal is known or unknown.

3. A certain receiver utilizes a square law detector, and currently $(p_f, p_d) = (.1, .9)$. What would be the effect on p_d if the signal power were doubled and the false alarm probability were held constant? Assume that

    10.1-4 holds and the signal is weak.

    ANSWER: Currently, $x = 1.28$ and $x - \sqrt{d} = -1.28$, so $\sqrt{d} = 2.56$. The effect of doubling signal power is to double $\sqrt{d}$ in this case, so the new detection probability is $1 - \Phi(-3.84) = .9999$. Note the high sensitivity of p_d to the signal level.

4. a) Using 10.1-4, find an expression for the dimensionless threshold x that minimizes 10.4-1.

   ANSWER: $x = \left[\ln\left(\dfrac{qc_2}{pc_1}\right) + \dfrac{d}{2} \right] \Big/ \sqrt{d}$

   b) Verify the exact answer in Exercise 1.

   c) Search is being conducted for objects that have a value of $100. For every target call an expendable device worth $1 must be used. The expendable device recovers the object if the target call is a detection, or else is wasted if the target call is a false alarm. If the detection index is 4.0, what is the optimal false alarm probability? Assume that an object is actually present on .0001 of the detection opportunities.

   ANSWER: $p_f = 1 - \Phi(3.3) = .0005$. The associated detection probability is $1 - \Phi(1.3) = .1$.

5. Using 10.1-4, graph the function $p_d/(1 + 10p_f)$ as a function of x to determine the maximum effective detection rate (Formula 10.4-2) when $d/\delta = 10$. Assume $d = 4$. What are the optimal values of p_f and p_d?

   ANSWER: The best x is about 1.725, with the optimal values for p_f and p_d being .0422 and .6084. The function is then .4278, which is maximal.

6. In Dobbie's two-cell example,

   $$b_i(t_i) = 1 - \exp(-t_i), \ \underline{\delta} = (0, 1), \ \underline{\tau} = (1, 1), \text{ and } \underline{p} = (.358, .632).$$

   Using 10.5-2, sketch a graph of the fraction of total search time devoted to cell one by the ONAP as a function of total search time.

   ANSWER: The sketch should pass through the point (2.95, .43).

7. Table 10-12 is a partial description of an ONAP. Compute an upper bound on T_{ONAP} for the same problem by computing T_{ENAP} from 10.5-4. Better yet, find a formula for T_{ENAP} when $\underline{p}$, $\underline{\delta}$, $\underline{\tau}$, and $\underline{\alpha}$ have the same meanings as in that example.

ANSWER: $T_{\text{ENAP}} = \Sigma(\lambda/\alpha_i + 5\delta_I\tau_i)$ in general, which reduces to 23/6 in the specific case. Note that T_{ENAP} is independent of $\underline{p}$; this makes the ENAP a particularly interesting plan if $\underline{p}$ is unknown or else is assumed to be worst case.

8. Sketch the curve referred to in the example of Section 10.6. To do that, it will be useful to employ sheet "Cascade" of the workbook *Search4.xls*.

REFERENCES

[1] Dobbie, J. 1973. Some search problems with false contacts. *Oper. Res.* **21** 907–925.

[2] Fechner, G. 1966. *Elements of Psychophysics.* Translated by Helmut Adler. Holt, Rinehart, and Winston, New York.

[3] Pollock, S. 1971. Search detection and subsequent action: Some problems on the interfaces. *Oper. Res.* **19** 559–586.

[4] Skolnik, M. 1980. *Introduction to Radar Systems.* McGraw-Hill, New York.

[5] Stone, L. 1975. *Theory of Optimal Search.* INFORMS, Linthicum, MD.

[6] Swets, J. 1964. *Signal Detection and Recognition by Human Observers.* Wiley, New York.

[7] Urick, R. 1975. *Principles of Underwater Sound for Engineers.* McGraw-Hill, New York.

11. THE STATISTICAL PROBLEM OF TRUNCATED TRIALS

A common statistical nightmare goes something as follows: A computer is programmed so that two people can play a search game, the idea being to keep track of the time T for A to capture B in repeated independent trials. After measuring the capture times, various statistical quantities such as the mean or the experimental CDF of T (Figure 2-8) are planned to be computed. Unfortunately, some of the trials are artificially terminated due to such unforeseen phenomena as computer breakdown, the need for one of the participants to visit the bathroom, etc. No capture time is recorded for such trials; only a truncation time is available.

The idea of simply ignoring all artificially terminated trials is not satisfactory. It would result in an estimate of the mean time to capture that is biased low, since truncations tend to occur for large values of the capture time. On the other hand, including the truncation times as if they were capture times is not the thing to do either, since this would again result in a low estimate. Even throwing out the whole experiment is no solution, since this policy would result in only experiments with no truncations (which tend to be experiments with low capture times) being recorded. The experimenter may come to feel that he has committed some essentially unpardonable statistical sin by permitting some of his trials to be truncated.

Fortunately, there are some reasonable estimating procedures even for experiments with truncated trials. Two of the more important of these (the reduced sample (RS) estimate and the product limit (PL) estimate) are discussed in [3] for problems where truncations prevent large observations, as in the problem described above. Truncations may also prevent small observations, as is characteristic of attempts to measure lateral range curves; the rest of this chapter will focus on them exclusively. The RS (Section 11.1) and PL (Section 11.2) estimates are both non-parametric. A different estimate based on the assumption that truncations are uniformly distributed is discussed in Section 11.3.

The following example will be used throughout. Assume that a sensor has associated with it a random detection range R. In order to measure the probability law of R, a sequence of experiments where a target travels a path that comes within X of the sensor is performed. On each experiment, the detection range is recorded if it exceeds X. The values of R in successive experiments are assumed to be independent of each other and the X's. Since $P(R \geq r)$ is the probability of detecting a target on a straight line path that comes within r of the sensor, measuring the probability law of R (which is the goal) is the same as measuring a lateral range curve. Also, $E(R)$ is half the sweepwidth. Table 11-2 shows R and X on five trials. Five trials is not very many, but a larger example would be tedious.

TRIAL	R	X
1	2	4
2	10	7
3	8	3
4	9	1
5	6	14

DETECTION RANGES AND CLOSEST POINTS OF APPROACH

11.1. The Reduced Sample (RS) Estimate

Let $P(r)$ be the true probability that the detection range is at least r. An estimate $\hat{P}(r)$ of $P(r)$ is to be made from the data. If all the data in Table 11-2 were available, the experimental distribution of the five detection ranges (the Standard Estimate) would and should be used to estimate $P(r)$. However, suppose that the truncation effect leaves only the data in Table 11-3, in which the values of R smaller than the corresponding values of X are not observed because the target never gets close enough.

TRIAL	R	X
1		4
2	10	7
3	8	3
4	9	1
5		14

TRUNCATING THE SMALL DETECTION RANGES

It is no longer possible to form the Standard Estimate. One could form the "Naive Estimate" by recording the experimental distribution only for those three trials where a detection range is observed, but the Naive Estimate is biased. This bias is evident in Figure 11-4, which compares the Naive and Standard Estimates in the top graph.

The RS Estimate is formed as follows. To estimate $P(5.5)$, include only those trials for which $X \leq 5.5$, since it is only those trials for which the question of whether $R \geq 5.5$ is definitely resolvable. These trials are 1, 3, and 4. Among these trials, $R \geq 5.5$ on trials 3 and 4, but not on trial 1 (in fact $R \leq 4$ on trial 1), so $\hat{P}(5.5) = 2/3$, the RS estimate of $P(r)$ for $r = 5.5$. It is important to note that trial 2 is not counted, even though $R \geq 5.5$ on that trial.

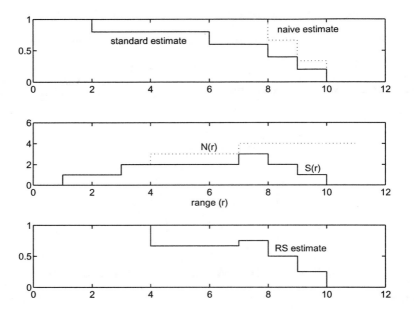

THE STANDARD, NAIVE, AND REDUCED SAMPLE ESTIMATES

More formally, let $N(r)$ be the number of trials for which $X \leq r$, and let $S(r)$ be the number of trials for which both $X \leq r$ and $R \geq r$. Then $\hat{P}(r) = S(r)/N(r)$ is the RS estimate as long as $N(r) > 0$. When $N(r) = 0$, $P(r)$ cannot be estimated because there have been no trials. The middle graph in Figure 11-4 shows $N(r)$ and $S(r)$ for the data in Table 11-5, and the bottom graph shows $\hat{P}(r)$. Note that $\hat{P}(r)$ is not decreasing, even though $P(r)$ has to be. Nonetheless, the RS estimate is known to be unbiased [11].

11.2. The Product Limit (PL) Estimate

Suppose now that the only data available are as in Table 11-5, which shows the situation where the closest point of approach is not known for those trials where a detection range is recorded. This is not uncommon. In exercises, for example, the sensor may take some action after detection such that the question of what the closest point of approach

11-4

would have been if there had been no detection is essentially unanswerable. The testing situation described in Section 11.1 is also of this type.

TRIAL	R	X
1		4
2	10	
3	8	
4	9	
5		14

REMOVING THE SMALL CPA'S FROM TABLE 11-3

The RS estimate cannot be made given only the data in Table 11-5, but the PL estimate of $P(r)$ can still be constructed. First, number the k detection ranges from smallest to largest (so $k = 3$, $R_1 = 8$, $R_2 = 9$, $R_3 = 10$). Let M_i be the number of recorded ranges (counting both R's and X's) that are $\leq R_i$ (so $M_1 = 2$, $M_2 = 3$, and $M_3 = 4$). Then estimate $\hat{P}(r)$ to be the smallest non-negative step function such that

$$
\begin{cases}
\hat{P}(R_k) = 1/M_k \\
\hat{P}(R_i) = \hat{P}(R_{i+1}) + \left[1 - \hat{P}(R_{i+1})\right]\Big/M_i, \quad i = 1,\dots,k-1.
\end{cases}
\tag{11.2-1}
$$

For values of r smaller than the smallest recorded range (again counting both R's and X's), $\hat{P}(r)$ is undefined.

Formula 11.2-1 defines the PL estimate. It can be justified as follows: There are a total of M_i trials for which the detection range is less than R_{i+1} and for which the closest point of approach is smaller than R_i. Of these, exactly one has a detection range $\geq R_i$. Therefore $\hat{P}(R \geq R_i | R < R_{i+1}) = 1/M_i$, and Formula 11.2-1 follows from the laws of conditional probability. The reason for requiring that the closest point of approach be smaller than R_i in selecting those trials from which

$P(R \geq R_i | R < R_{i+1})$ is to be estimated is that the question of whether

$R \geq R_i$ is not definitely resolvable otherwise. The reader who is suspicious of arguments such as this may take comfort in knowing that the PL estimate can also be shown to be maximum likelihood in the space of all distribution functions [3].

Figure 11-6 shows the PL estimate for the data in Table 11-3. The PL estimate is non-increasing, as should be clear from Formula 11.2-1. Other properties are discussed in [5], and Route [4] gives a favorable report based on testing by computer simulation.

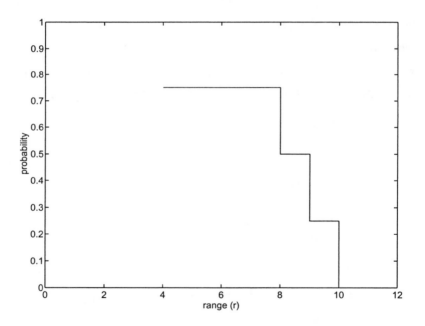

EXAMPLE OF PRODUCT LIMIT ESTIMATE

11.3. The Case of No CPA Records

Previous parts of this chapter have dealt with successively diminished versions of the data base. It is logical to next consider the case where no records whatever are available on closest point of approach. This would be natural for non-cooperative targets. All that is recorded is a succession of detection ranges; the trials for which lateral range exceeds detection range leave no trace whatever. All that is to be estimated is the (half) sweepwidth $E(R)$.

The truncation phenomenon is still present. Short detection ranges are unlikely to be recorded compared to long ones, so simply averaging the recorded detection ranges would produce an estimate of half sweepwidth that is biased high.

Each trial is characterized by a detection range R and an independent lateral range X, with R being recorded only in the event D that $X \le R$. Assume that R has a density function $f_R(r)$ and a conditional density function $f_{R|D}(r)$. By conditional probability,

$$P(R \le r|D)P(D) = \int_0^r P(D|R = x)f_R(x)dx$$

$$= \int_0^r P(X \le x)f_R(x)dx.$$

(11.3-1)

Now assume that X is typically large relative to R; more precisely, assume that the density function of X is approximately constant over the interval for which $f_R(x)$ is significantly positive. If this constant is K, then Kx can be substituted for $P(X \le x)$ in 11.3-1, which produces

$$P(R \le r|D)P(D) = K\int_0^r xf_R(x)dx .$$

(11.3-2)

Substituting $r = \infty$ into 11.3-2,

$$P(D) = KE(R).$$

(11.3-3)

Solving 11.3-3 for K and substituting into 11.3-2, we obtain

$$P(R \leq r|D)E(R) = \int_0^r x f_R(x)dx . \tag{11.3-4}$$

Differentiating 11.3-4 with respect to r,

$$f_{R|D}(r)E(R) = r f_R(r) . \tag{11.3-5}$$

From 11.3-5, it follows that

$$E(1/R|D) = \int_0^\infty \left(\frac{1}{r}\right) f_{R|D}(r)dr = \frac{1}{E(R)} \int_0^\infty f_R(r)dr = \frac{1}{E(R)} . \tag{11.3-6}$$

Since $E(1/R|D)$ can be estimated from the recorded detection ranges, so can $E(R)$ by taking the reciprocal. Specifically, if $R_1, ..., R_n$ are the recorded detection ranges, then $\overline{(1/R)} \equiv (1/R_1 + ...+ 1/R_n)/n$ is an unbiased estimate of $1/E(R)$, so $\overline{(1/R)}^{-1}$ could be used as an estimate of $E(R)$. The quantity $\overline{(1/R)}^{-1}$ is the <u>harmonic mean</u> of the measured detection ranges.

Normally (without truncation), one would estimate $E(R)$ using the familiar <u>arithmetic</u> mean $\overline{R} \equiv (R_1 + ...+ R_n)/n$ to estimate $E(R)$. When only large ranges can be observed, however, it is better to use the harmonic mean $\overline{(1/R)}^{-1}$. The harmonic mean will always be smaller than the arithmetic mean unless all recorded ranges are equal.

To continue with the example used throughout this section, suppose only the measured detection ranges on trials 2, 3, and 4 from Table 11-5 were available. Then the harmonic mean estimate of $E(R)$ would be $3/(1/10 + 1/8 + 1/9) = 8.93$. This is only slightly smaller than the arithmetic mean 9.00; the contrast would be more striking if the measured detection ranges had more variance.

This section has dealt only with sweepwidth estimation, but an estimate of the lateral range curve itself is actually possible [1].

11.4. Hypothesis Testing

This section deals with the problem of deciding whether a given probability law provides a good enough fit to data measured in a succession of occasionally truncated trials. This goal differs from the estimation goal in previous parts of Section 11, where no such probability law was given.

Let there be n trials, with the ith trial of maximum length t_i, and assume that the ith trial measures whether the amount of time T_i required to detect a target exceeds t_i or not. If $T_i \leq t_i$, then a detection occurs. Let F_i be the postulated CDF of T_i; that is, $P(T_i \leq t) = F_i(t)$. Since $F_i(t_i)$ is the probability of detection on the ith trial, $\sum_{i=1}^{n} F_i(t_i)$ is the average number of detections in n trials. If N is the measured number of detections in n trials, a natural statistic to investigate is the Bernoulli statistic

$$S_n = \left(N - \sum_{i=1}^{n} F_i(t_i) \right) \Big/ n . \qquad (11.4\text{-}1)$$

If F_i is truly the CDF of T_i for all i (the null hypothesis H_0), then $E(S_n) = 0$, so the extent to which S_n differs from zero can be used to accept (if $|S_n|$ is small) or reject (if $|S_n|$ is large) H_0. A difficulty may arise, however, if the ith trial is terminated at detection. There is no problem as long as $F_i(t_i)$ can still be evaluated, but the function F_i may very well depend on the relative positions of searcher and target, in which case one has to face the question of what the relative positions would have been after T_i for trials on which a detection occurs. In the event that this question is unanswerable, a new statistic is required. Bossard [2] recommends the following, assuming F_i is continuous:

Let

$$\hat{P}_i = \begin{cases} F_i(t_i) & \text{if } T_i > t_i \\ 2F_i(T_i) & \text{if } T_i \le t_i. \end{cases} \tag{11.4-2}$$

Note that knowledge of $F_i(t)$ for $t > T_i$ is not required to evaluate $\hat{P}_i$.

Furthermore, assuming H_0,

$$E(\hat{P}_i) = \int_0^{t_i} 2F(t)\,dF(t) + \int_{t_i}^{\infty} F(t_i)\,dF(t)$$

$$= F^2(t_i) + F(t_i)(1 - F(t_i)) \tag{11.4-3}$$

$$= F(t_i).$$

Let $\hat{S}_n$ be defined by

$$\hat{S}_n = \left(N - \sum_{i=1}^{n} \hat{P}_i\right)\Big/ n. \tag{11.4-4}$$

Then $E(\hat{S}_n) = 0$, so $\hat{S}_n$ can be used to test H_0, just as S_n was used in the case of no truncations. The question of significance levels is taken up in [2], along with a Kolmogorov-Smirnov type of statistic. It is also pointed out in [2] that it is not necessary to assume $F_i(t)$ is continuous, although the definition of P_i must be altered somewhat. Also, the numbers t_i may be random variables, as long as t_i is independent of T_i.

CHAPTER 11. Exercises

1. Consider the detection range (R) and lateral range (X) data shown in the table below, and let $P(r) = P(R \geq r)$.

TRIAL	R	X
1	2	9
2	3	1
3	3	5
4	6	4
5	7	5
6	8	5

a) What is the normal estimate of $P(r)$?

b) Cross out R in those cases where $R < x$ and make the RS estimate of $P(r)$.

c) Cross out the smaller number in each row and make the PL estimate of $P(r)$.

d) Cross out R in those cases where $R < X$ and also the whole X column. Estimate sweepwidth using the harmonic mean of the remaining detection ranges.

ANSWER: a) a graph for which $\hat{P}(3.5) = .5$

b) a graph for which $\hat{P}(3.5) = 0$

c) a graph for which $\hat{P}(3.5) = .6$

d) $1344/129 = 10.4$

2. Suppose that detection ranges are uniform in the interval $[0,10]$ and lateral ranges are uniform in the interval $[0,20]$. Using a random number generator or a table of random numbers, simulate several trials and compare either the RS estimate or the PL estimate with $P(r) = 1 - r/10$. Alternatively, compare the harmonic mean estimate

with the actual sweepwidth. Writing a computer program to do the computations would be instructive and would permit "several trials" to be (say) 1000 instead of only (say) 10.

REFERENCES

[1] Arnold, R. D., J. Bram. 1962. Estimating the lateral range curve from observed detection ranges. IRM-27, Center for Naval Analyses, Washington, DC.

[2] Bossard, D. C. 1970. Statistical tests for detection models. Daniel H. Wagner Associates, Paoli, PA.

[3] Kaplan, E. L., P. Meier. 1958. Nonparameteric estimation from incomplete observations. *J. Amer. Statist. Assoc.* **53** 457–481.

[4] Route, R. A. 1976. An investigation of the applicability of the product limit estimate to the statistical analysis of sonar detection distributions. Naval Postgraduate School Thesis.

[5] Spitz, H. 1964. Estimating cumulative probability from aggregated truncated data. Operations Evaluation Group Research Contribution 56, Center for Naval Analyses.